Testimonials

Email marketing, alongside search marketing, still tops many surveys of the most effective digital channel. Marketers use it with enthusiasm because it's effective and relatively cheap, quick and easy compared to other channels. But often, the full potential of email marketing is missed and businesses aren't tapping into the insights and the automation tools available to deliver more contextual, responsive emails. Perhaps it's too quick and easy, so it's not treated as strategically?

In *E-telligence* Kate Barrett clearly shows how to audit your current approach to develop an email and data strategy to deliver better email marketing results for a business. I love the tables in the book which will help you review your approach plus the prompts of how to take action. I also enjoyed the case studies from different sectors which show how the strategies recommended can be used in practice.

Dr. Dave Chaffey – Co-founder and Content Director, SmartInsights.com

Email marketing might not be rocket science, but if you're building a team of partners to help you optimise your programme, having the equivalent of a rocket scientist on your side will go a long way – this book gives you the scientist and the fuel!

Bill Kaplan – CEO, FreshAddress & leader of the MIT Blackjack Team

Kate knows a lot about email! In an industry that draws from many skill sets, Kate is that rarest of things – a jack of all trades, and *master of all*.

Guy Hanson – Vice President of Global Professional Services, Return Path & Chair of the DMA (UK) Email Council

E-telligence

Email marketing isn't dead,
THE WAY YOU'RE USING IT IS

Kate Barrett

Printed in the United Kingdom
First Printing, 2019

ISBN: 978-1-9164894-0-0 (Print edition)
ISBN: 978-1-9164894-1-7 (eBook Edition)

Librotas Books
Portsmouth, Hampshire
UK
PO2 9NT

www.Librotas.com

Contents

Testimonials   1

Foreword   7

Introduction   9

CHAPTER 1: KNOW What You've Already Got   15

1.1: Send Strategy   21

1.2: Data   31

1.3: Segmentation and Personalisation   42

1.4: Automated Campaign Strategy   51

1.5: Design   57

1.6: Results Tracking   65

1.7: Testing Strategy   71

1.8: Technology and Processes   78

CHAPTER 2: IMPROVE What You're Doing   91

2.1: Send Strategy   93

2.2: Data   104

2.3: Segmentation and Personalisation   117

2.4: Automated Campaign Strategy   134

2.5: Design   148

2.6: Results Tracking   169

2.7: Testing Strategy   173

2.8: Technology and Processes   181

CHAPTER 3: FILL IN Your Gaps   193

3.1: Optimising Your Email Marketing Strategy   195

3.2: Enhancing the Customer Journey   202

3.3: Multichannel Marketing   225

CHAPTER 4: GROW Your Audience   229

4.1: Quantifying Your Email List   231
4.2: Your Current Sign-Up Process   238
4.3: Optimising Your Sign-Up Form to Maximise Conversions   247
4.4: Making Your Opt-In Attractive   252
4.5: Post-Sign-Up Strategy   254
4.6: Advertise Your Opt-In   256

CHAPTER 5: REACH Your Audience   267

5.1: Your Sender Reputation   269
5.2: Your Sending IP Address   282

Email marketing isn't dead, the way you're using it is...   291

Acknowledgements   293

About eFocus Marketing   294

Appendices   295

References   313

Foreword

Forty years after the first use of marketing emails, the channel is still consistently ranked as the most effective method for companies to communicate with their customers.

Email is regularly cited by consumers as their preferred method of contact by brands. In turn, marketers love email because of its ease of testing, its measurability, and the near-real-time responses that it generates. It also helps that email is a great driver of Return-on-Investment (ROI), with Direct Marketing Association reports regularly citing returns of £30:1 or higher!

Which poses the question – 'Why isn't email being used even more?'

There are several answers. One is that for all its benefits, email also comes with limitations, with some of the most frequently cited including: limited resource; limited budget; lack of data; lack of strategy; outdated technology and inefficient processes. Aligned with these, many email practitioners still struggle to prove the value of their programmes, making it hard to prepare strong business cases to secure additional investment. Email is also an incredibly fast-moving space – it's really hard to stay up to speed with the near-constant evolutions in technology, industry standards, best practices, and legislation.

What email marketers need is a book – like this one!

I've known Kate Barrett for many years now – as a customer, as a strategic consultant (including for my own team), as a DMA email councillor, and as an entrepreneur.

She is truly one of a kind, for several reasons:

- Kate's sheer passion for email. It gets her up in the morning, and I suspect she dreams about it at night. A mutual client once referred to Kate as 'the Mother Theresa of email!'

- Secondly, Kate knows a lot about email! In an industry that draws from many skill sets, Kate is that rarest of things – a jack of all trades, and *master of all*.

- And finally, Kate is a natural storyteller. She has the ability to process complex data, and turn it into a set of actionable, easy-to-understand learnings that her clients can apply to their email programmes.

I list these attributes because, as you read through this book, you will realise what a great job Kate has done re-creating them for a reading audience. Her knowledge, enthusiasm, and practical guidance come through on every page – making it not just a valuable and informative read, but a thoroughly entertaining one too!

Guy Hanson
Vice President of Global Professional Services, Return Path
Chair of the DMA (UK) Email Council

Introduction

'Email Marketing is Dead'

This rumour has been constantly debated since I started working in the industry over a decade ago – but if anything, email marketing is thriving and becoming an even more critical part of your marketing strategy.

Email marketing underpins all your other marketing efforts by taking prospects from just becoming aware of your brand as a result of other marketing channels (such as social media, print advertising or search engine marketing), to developing a relationship with them so that they become loyal customers and advocates.

Email is integral to most, if not all, modern marketing campaign strategies – according to the DMA Email Marketer Tracker Report (2018) 86% of respondents rated it as very important to their organisation. (Source: DMA Email Marketer Tracker Report 2018[1])

It's the perfect fit for any business wanting to build a relationship with subscribers and generate revenue. Whether you are Business-to-Business (B2B) or Business-to-Consumer (B2C) focused, email marketing can be effectively used to engage and convert subscribers as well as to drive direct sales for your business.

But you have to be using it in the right way – intelligently and with a customer-first focus.

Organisations achieving the highest results from this channel are those who are using email intelligently; gone are the days of batch and blast, sending the same thing to everyone and expecting to make the highest returns.

Nowadays, you have to get clever with the communications you're sending and make sure that your potential customers' needs, wants and desires are put at the forefront of your strategy, in order for you to stand out.

But it can be hard as a marketer – you're probably juggling lots of different marketing channels and email is just one (crucially important) part of that wider strategy.

Like many others, you may be struggling with:

- a lack of strategy
- limited internal resources
- inefficient internal processes
- outdated technology
- a lack of content
- limited budgets

This book aims to help you overcome the most significant of these challenges – a lack of strategy – and create a solid foundation for a wildly successful email marketing programme.

You've probably picked this book up because you want to improve your knowledge – perhaps like many of us you haven't been formally trained or taught how to plan, implement and optimise campaigns in the best possible way. You've been expected to figure it out for yourself or have picked up little bits from historical work/team members.

You know you could be doing so much more with your campaigns.

You want to learn more and take your organisation's email marketing to the next level, or even give a boost to your own career prospects!

But you may not know where to start and how to focus your limited time and resources.

In this book I will teach you to use email marketing more intelligently – hence **'E-telligence'**!

Putting the customer at the heart of everything you do

This means prioritising the needs and wants of your subscribers before those of your company – trust me, in return, you'll benefit from increased engagement, conversions and revenue by working in this way.

Throughout this book we'll talk about various ways to do this – from knowing exactly who your potential customers are and their desires, to collecting the right information to be able to identify these needs (sometimes before they even know themselves!) and using it to inform your strategy and content.

I've been working in email marketing for well over ten years – at a strategic level, as well as being in the trenches day-to-day, working on creating and optimising campaigns.

I've been a judge for the DMA awards over multiple years, a member of the DMA Email Council for over three years, a regular speaker at events around the world, and have also been lucky enough to work on a range of projects for companies of all sizes, from entrepreneurs just getting started, to large multinational companies including Nissan, Adidas, QVC, Neal's Yard Remedies, Marks & Spencer, TUI, Argos and many more.

From strategic reviews to campaign execution and everything in between, I've been where you are, I've walked in your shoes and still do today for my clients.

I understand the struggles you face, not only to plan successful campaigns, but to attain the resources to execute them. The lack of senior support in some cases, poor interdepartmental communication, frustrating technology issues and outdated systems are all struggles that I've experienced over the years.

I've written this book to give you a roadmap through the five key stages to making a positive impact on your email marketing campaigns and taking your strategy to the next level:

Step 1 – KNOW What You've Got
Step 2 – IMPROVE What You're Doing
Step 3 – FILL IN Your Gaps
Step 4 – GROW Your Audience
Step 5 – REACH Your Audience

So, if you want to improve your knowledge and career prospects, or help your team have a deeper understanding of what makes a successful strategy, you're in the right place!

By the time you've reached the end of this book, you'll have conducted an audit of your current strategy to give you a clear view of where you are coming from, know how to optimise what you're currently doing, have a plan of how you will move forward to increase the ROI of your campaigns over the next 6–12 months, as well as a clearer understanding of how deliverability works and the importance of consistently growing your email list.

At the end of each section you'll find a **'TAKE ACTION'** prompt with various tasks.

These are here to help you act on the knowledge you are gaining as you work your way through each chapter. Without implementing what you are learning you won't see positive changes in your programme, so it's important you complete these as you go.

Your Online Resources

As an accompaniment to this book, I have also created an online membership portal that has a wealth of additional resources for you to draw on that will help you work through the information I'm about to share with you:

- A range of downloads to help you complete many of the tasks in the book
- Videos to support and expand on some of the best practices discussed, including real-life examples to inspire you
- A place to submit your questions and seek advice from the community
- Videos from our sponsors showing how their tools can help you successfully implement many of the strategies and tactics featured

And much more!

Simply go to www.etelligencebook.com/
and register using the code **'ETELLIGENCE'** to gain access.

So, let's get stuck into Chapter 1 and start uncovering the details of your current strategy so that you know you have a solid foundation on which to build.

CHAPTER 1

KNOW
What You've Already Got

In order to start improving your email marketing strategy, the best place to focus your attention is not on what's new and fancy or shiny, but on what you're already doing.

You're probably already using email marketing to varying degrees of success within your business.

But do you know exactly what you're sending, when and to whom?

Is it well documented and consistently reviewed?

If you have a programme just sending a couple of promotional emails a week to your list, for example, and nothing much else, you may be pretty confident that you do know exactly what you already have in place.

For those with more complex programmes already in place, even if you think you do, it's so easy to miss something. For example, to not realise exactly how a trigger is working, that an email isn't sending when/to whom you thought it was, or an unsubscribe link isn't working.

Whichever end of the scale you're at, I want you to start your journey to an amazingly successful, comprehensive email programme on the right foot, by **knowing EXACTLY where you are now** and, more importantly, **where you want to go next.**

The way to do this is to conduct an audit of your current strategy before you jump into any optimisation or addition of new campaigns (individual emails or a series of emails that work towards achieving your goals).

'You can't know where you're going until you know where you've been.'

Conducting an audit – a full review of exactly what's happening with your email marketing right now – can seem like a big task.

But it is absolutely critical to help you pinpoint the areas where you're not best serving your subscribers, and fill those gaps to create a better programme, as well as increase your results.

This audit document is something you should regularly keep up-to-date and be checking in with – a 'living document' if you will.

It will be something that other team members can pick up and understand exactly what's going on in your business, and can be updated as you introduce additional campaigns to your strategy or pinpoint key learnings.

It will keep you moving forward and ensure you see results.

I've worked for many brands in the past and know what it's like when you have so many responsibilities in your day-to-day role but also have senior management pressuring for more results, faster!

This document will help you to manage all of that and more. It will allow you to see the results of the work you are doing and provide a record, a baseline, for your next move.

So, where do you start?

The aim of the audit is not only to create a documented record of your current strategy, but also to **pinpoint areas of strength and weakness in your current programme.**

Using this information, you can then find solutions to problems (some you may not even have known existed, such as information being outdated) and improve your results.

To analyse your programme, you'll need to pull together a wealth of data, including:

- campaign and segment performance data, including all statistics available to you such as opens, clicks, complaints, unsubscribes and conversion data.

- a list of all campaigns set up to send to subscribers. Don't forget that these may not all be in one ESP (Email Service Provider – the technology you are using to create and send your emails); some may be triggered from internal systems, your CRM (Customer Relationship Management system) or your eCommerce platform, for example. Make sure you ask other people in your organisation (specifically IT) about ANY emails that are sent to subscribers.

  You'll also need to get:
  o screenshots of each of these emails
  o campaign details (such as when the emails are sent and the main purpose of them)
  o why they are sent from each system (if applicable – for example, transactional emails sent from your eCommerce platform may be set up in this way as there is not currently a link between it and your ESP)
  o and any other information that will allow you to analyse what you already have in place.

- different responses to your programme within the business. To do this, conduct a questionnaire with different departments (for example, customer services) and find out what their experience of the company email programme has been, as well as any feedback, comments or complaints they have received from customers and prospects about it. What do they think needs to be changed/added to make the communications better?

- your subscribers' view of your current campaigns – send a short questionnaire to subscribers or use an in-email poll to gain valuable feedback! What do they most like/dislike about your emails? Do they find them interesting and relevant? Are they too long? Ask questions that will help to delve into the mind of the customer and use this information at each stage of your audit to better understand the impact different areas have in real life. But don't forget to keep it short; no one likes long surveys so try and keep it to 5 questions or less in order to maximise response.

Over the following eight sections of this chapter, we'll evaluate the key areas of your programme, drawing on the knowledge you've gathered from these sources.

The areas we will look at include:

Follow this as a framework of key elements to analyse when reviewing your current strategy.

The additional section you should also be evaluating is your list acquisition process – we will look at this separately in Chapter 4.

 **TAKE ACTION**

As you work through each section in this chapter, rate yourself with a score between 0 and 10 for each of the eight areas depending on how you view your programme now (with 0 being no strategy in place within that area, and 10 being a complete, comprehensive strategy with no improvements needed).

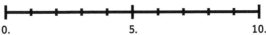

0.	**5.**	**10.**
Nothing at all present in this area	Some elements present, but room for improvement	No further improvement in this area possible

Strategic Area	Score
1. Send Strategy	
2. Data	
3. Segmentation and Personalisation	
4. Automated Campaign Strategy	
5. Design	
6. Results Tracking	
7. Testing Strategy	
8. Technology and Processes	
TOTAL (out of 80)	

This will highlight the areas where you have the most work to do.

It is also useful as a benchmark to come back to as you improve each section, and to monitor your progress going forward.

You can download a copy of this chart to fill in for your business here:
www.etelligencebook.com/members/step1/benchmark/

1.1
Send Strategy

'A goal without a plan is just a wish.'
– Antoine de Saint-Exupéry

As I mentioned in the Introduction, a lack of strategy is **one of the most significant challenges to successfully executing email marketing programmes** and is the first place to start when it comes to reviewing your current processes.

Do You Have a Clear, Documented Email Marketing Strategy?

Having a documented plan of where you want to go and how you're going to get there is essential and can offer a multitude of benefits.

A well thought-out strategy will allow you to:

- identify your best customers and help you to better understand their needs.

- implement the most relevant and targeted campaigns to gain the best possible results.

- identify prospects/customers at different stages of the customer journey, giving you insights into how best to serve their needs with the aim of moving them further towards making an initial or repeat purchase.

- measure, monitor and continuously improve what you are doing.

- stay focused, motivated, and accountable.

A strategy is simply knowing where you want to go and how you plan to get there – ideas that can be turned into actions.

You therefore need to be able to detail the following information in order to develop and implement email marketing activities successfully:

- **Goals** – do you know what your goals are within the business and for each email campaign you send? What do you want to achieve with your email marketing? How does it tie in to the overall business strategy and goals? What is the purpose of email marketing for your company?

- **Tactics** – what resources will you need? How are you going to achieve your goals and implement your strategy? What type of campaigns will you send?

  What kind of tests will you run? At what stages during the customer journey will these campaigns be sent? (The customer journey will be discussed in more detail in the next chapter.) How will you use personalisation within your strategy to really connect with your audience? Will you use mobile-responsive designs? How will you bring value to your subscribers?

- **Specific actions** – when will you send individual campaigns? What will the key elements of campaigns include? What offers will you include? What subject lines will you use? Who will be responsible for running your campaigns? What will the content of each email be? When will you run your tests?

- **Results** – how will you measure success? How will you calculate Return-on-Investment (ROI)? What other metrics will you record and analyse to demonstrate success?

I'll go into more detail about each of these areas in the next chapter and how you build on them, but first it's vital you gain a clear understanding of exactly what you have in place within your business RIGHT NOW, so that you can then organise this into a more detailed plan to improve performance going forward.

Your strategy will contain multiple campaigns but it all starts with knowing WHY you are sending them – what you want to achieve. Everything else can be mapped backwards from there to detail the tactics and actions needed to get you there.

These tactics will be divided out into various areas, many of which we will cover in the following sections of this chapter, and in this book as a whole.

Manual Campaigns vs. Triggered Campaigns

Within your strategy you will have two types of email marketing campaigns you are sending – those that are date-based and physically built and sent each day/week/month, and then there are those that are built in advance within your ESP and sent automatically in response to a subscriber action (or inaction in some cases), based on data you hold.

For example, sending your weekly promotional email, advertising a range of products every Tuesday, is a *manual email*.

An abandoned basket campaign, automated to send to a subscriber when they leave an item(s) in their basket without going on to purchase, is a *triggered campaign* (also known as an *automated campaign*, *drip campaign* or *follow-up*).

Yearly Send Plan

When it comes to your manual campaigns, it is vital to have a clear plan for what you will be sending, when and why, in order to stay on track, ensure you have the right resources in place to fulfil your plans and continue to generate revenue from your email marketing.

The best way to do this is to have a calendar of sends for your email marketing that documents when each email is being sent and why, as well as the key details of the campaign and what you want to achieve.

I will take you through creating your send plan in the 'Take Action' section in Chapter 2.1, but for now, consider and take note of any plans you already have in place to map out these types of emails and when you will send them.

Your Content

Not only is it important to ensure *HOW* you write your emails resonates with your subscribers and catches their attention in order to drive the desired action, but also that *WHAT* you're writing about is interesting and relevant.

When reviewing your current send strategy, think about the type of content you send out – is it what subscribers expect to receive? Do you personalise content based on their individual needs? Are you ensuring that your content is not repetitive?

In the following chapters of this book, I will discuss how you can tailor your content using **persona marketing** (developing customer personas so that you know exactly who you are targeting and what makes them 'tick'), **segmentation** (taking different sections of your list that have commonalities and targeting them specifically with relevant offers and information) and **personalisation** (using the data you have about individual subscribers to speak to them in a highly relevant way). All of this will help you create content that really connects with your subscribers.

How Subscribers View Your Email Marketing

You should always seek to step into your subscribers' shoes when looking at your strategy. Think about what their experience will be with what you are sending and how often you are sending it.

Will they find it relevant and interesting or is it a repetitive stream of promotions that don't have any relation to what they actually need?

Are you using your data in a way that means the content they receive and when they receive it is tailored to their specific situation, or are you sending the same thing to everyone regardless?

The more you can put your subscribers' individual needs at the forefront of your strategy, the higher the results you will see.

 # ✎ TAKE ACTION

Let's get clear on exactly what you have in place already and start creating your documented strategy.

You will continue to build on this as we go through each section of this chapter, to audit what you currently have, and onwards as you start to expand your strategy through the next four chapters.

If you already have a strategy document created within your business, I urge you to use the information we are covering here to recap what's already written and add to it where possible. The more information you have, the better informed your decisions will be going forward.

Your Current Strategy

- Thinking about each of the following areas, detail what you currently have in place in your business and answer the questions that were outlined for each earlier in this section.
  - o Goals
  - o Tactics
  - o Specific actions
  - o Results

Add as much detail as possible about the campaigns you currently have running (don't worry about the individual emails in each series for now; just think about the overall type – for example, abandoned basket email series. We'll delve deeper into individual email specifics in the next step of this task) and ensure that each one is listed against a goal.

Please see Appendix 1 on page 296 for an example.

This exercise will give you a quick overview of what's currently in place and why.

If you have a more comprehensive programme with multiple campaigns already in place the layout shown probably won't work for you. In this case, create a document that details this information in a format that suits you.

Or perhaps you do already have this documented in your business – brilliant! Make sure you review it at this stage and ensure that all the details are in place.

Ask yourself this question: *'If I were a new employee to the business, could I pick up this document and quickly see a summary of what campaigns are in place and why?'*

Plotting each campaign you currently send against the goal it represents is the most important element of this task – knowing WHY you are sending each campaign (what's the outcome you want to achieve?).

- The next step, as you go deeper into creating your email marketing strategy plan, is to create different sections of your document that go into more detail about each individual campaign.

As you do this consider detailing the following information:
  o Campaign type (manual vs. triggered)
  o Campaign name (for example, abandoned basket campaign)
  o What is the purpose of the campaign (overall goal)?
  o What are the individual emails that form part of this campaign?
  o Specific details of each email (for example, send timing, screenshots of emails contained, exclusions – who is included/ not included in these sends, any tests that have been previously run and their learnings, etc.)

You can download a worksheet for this exercise here:
www.etelligencebook.com/members/step1/sendstrategy/

Yearly Send Plan

- If you haven't already, ensure you have a documented plan of what you are going to send and when over the next 12 months for your manual campaigns.

This document may change in its detail as you go through the year (and new campaigns may be added), but you should have an overall idea of the majority of your campaigns in advance, even if you are not 100% sure of all the details of each yet.

As you get closer to each send date, you can fill in more information.

MONTH	Planned Campaigns
January	Date: Email marketing goal: Campaign outline: Call-to-action: Test details: Measure of success:
February	
March	
April	
May	
June	
July	
August	
September	
October	

MONTH	Planned Campaigns
November	
December	

You can download a copy of this to fill in for your business here:
www.etelligencebook.com/members/step1/yearlysendplan/

Your Content

- Consider the content you create for each of the types of manual campaign you listed above and answer the following questions:

  o Do you have running content themes or different types of email that you send regularly, such as a monthly newsletter, promotional mailings or weekly roundups? If not, could you implement this (perhaps just for specific segments)? Do you have regular send days for each of these different types of content? (For example, weekly roundup email on a Saturday or a month start/end newsletter.)

- Do you have a 'content bucket' plan with different categories of email content ideas? (We'll talk more about this in the next chapter, but essentially it is a pot of different content ideas that you can rotate between to prevent subscribers from getting bored by the same thing being sent to them in every email.)

- Do you regularly change up the focus of your emails to keep them fresh and interesting?

- Do you consider what content you are sending and to whom in order to ensure it resonates specifically with different types of subscribers?

- Do you stick to your brand tone of voice in communications?

- What types of content have been most successful (and for which segments)? Why do you think that is?

- What types of content have been least successful (and for which segments)? Why do you think that is?

- Are there any gaps in the content you are providing that would be helpful/interesting for your subscribers?

How Subscribers View Your Email Marketing

Think about the following questions:

- What information can you provide about your products/services that will help subscribers make the decision to buy/find out more?

- What content can you create that will tease or excite them?

- What questions might they have surrounding your products/ services that you could answer with your content? Refer back to any feedback you have received from other teams within your company and directly from your subscribers (in the form of surveys or in-email poll results for example). Are there any points here that you can pick up on that are particularly positive and those that are negative and need to be addressed within your programme?

1.2

Data

If it's in your database, you can use it to personalise, segment, target and trigger highly engaging emails.

Creating great email marketing begins with having and using great data. Knowing who you are speaking to is critical in order to create content that interests or motivates them as well as meeting their needs, and encouraging engagement. This starts with knowing exactly who you want to attract onto your database and collecting the right data by which to further target them.

In this section, we break down the different types of data you have so that you can start to build on your current database in a more strategic way. At the same time, you will be reviewing what data you already collect from each of these types and where it is stored in your business.

Types of Data

There are five main groups of data you can collect to learn more about your subscribers.

These are:

1. **Known Data**
   This is data collected directly from asking the subscriber, including details such as date of birth, address, company size and their preferences, for example demographic and interest data.

2. Behavioural Data

Tracking subscriber behaviour on your website using a dropped pixel and cookie tracking can give you a wealth of information about what your prospect needs RIGHT NOW: products they browse (categories, subcategories or individual products), blog posts they read, videos they watch and any other actions they take on your website (such as searches they perform); these will all tell you what they are actively looking for.

For example, if someone is browsing your FAQs, they are telling you with this behaviour that they are looking for more help. If they are looking at multiple products of the same type, they are trying to choose which is right for them. If they are browsing multiple categories they may be looking for inspiration.

This can also be as simple as identifying the lead magnet they chose that incentivised the sign-up – for example, a first order discount amount, free download, webinar sign-up or gaining access to a free video series.

This alone will give you an abundance of information about what the customer is interested in – for example, the topic of the free download they choose, the format of information they prefer and where they are in their research. If they are signing up for a first order discount, for example, they may be closer to considering making a purchase from you or be price sensitive.

All of this will inform how you can best serve them additional content to move them through the buying process.

3. Purchase Data

This will include information such as what, when and how many times they've purchased from you previously.

You could also extend this to conduct a full RFM analysis, ranking customers by the *Recency* with which they last bought from you, how *Frequently* they buy from you, and the amount of *Money* they spend. This allows you to identify your low, medium and high value customers and target them appropriately with offers depending on each of these elements.

4. **Contextual Data**

This includes information about what's happening for them right now, such as where they are (geographically), what device they are using to open their email, the current weather conditions or the time of day.

Real-time content involves content within your emails that personalises at the moment a subscriber opens the email such as:

o countdown timer
o weather forecasts/change imagery based on the weather
o maps
o polls
o trackers (delivery)
o live social media feeds

If you are a retailer with multiple shops on the high street around the country, for example, you may include a map in one of your email campaigns. The map shows the location of the shop closest to the subscriber when they open the email. Using geo-targeting, this map would change, within the same email, if the subscriber then opened it again in a different part of the country, to show the nearest store to their current location.

5. **Cultural Data**

This is data that surrounds your wider information – such as connecting different products together (by category, by type, by relevancy, by upsell/cross-sell options for example), or knowing what type of products are most relevant to people in different areas of the country. For example, if you're a supermarket, the products you advertise and which are attractive to people in Scotland or Wales or

England will be slightly different depending on the specific region, tastes and trends.

By bringing these types of data together, you can identify markers that allow you to discover the type of prospect they are, what they need from you and how you can best help them to move forward, helping you **understand and process** the information into a meaningful picture.

This is most useful when you can create a **single customer view** – where all the data you hold about each of your customers is stored and consolidated into one single, easy to read record in your database.

This should also include data pulled from all other marketing channels.

A true single customer view means being able to use this huge amount of data in a meaningful way to create a fuller, personalised picture of the customer and their journey. By doing so, you will be able to improve future interactions with customers and provide a more targeted, cohesive experience through a greater insight into customers' behaviours and interactions.

Conducting Your Data Audit

The first place to start building this picture is to review exactly which of these types of data you have about subscribers, in the business as a whole, and what is specifically available for email marketing purposes.

Then you can ascertain what you need and what you are missing to identify the data gaps.

The questions you should ask yourself in order to analyse this are:

1. **What data do you currently have?**
   List out all the data you currently collect directly from subscribers or track and record from different sources (these are described as data fields).

2. **Where is this data found within your business?**
   Are you currently collecting this data in other areas of the business but it's not currently linked to your email subscriber list?

   If you are, why is this data not available in your email marketing system, and could it be made available for use?

   Make a list of all the different systems within your business in which data may be stored, such as your ESP, CRM (customer relationship management system), POS (point of sale software), website software, additional marketing channels and other systems.

   Speak to the other departments within your business to ensure you have a clear picture of ALL data available and where it is currently stored (and why – are they using it for something that isn't related to email marketing?).

3. **Which pieces of this data are you currently using within your campaigns?**
   Identify the data you're currently using in your email programme, how you are using it and why. For example, to identify specific segments for increased relevancy (who is contacted, or not, as part of the current send strategy) or to personalise content with customer information (for example, pulling first name or the name of the last product purchased into your email content).

4. **Prioritise the data you have, based on value to your company and email marketing programme**

   Some data will be more valuable than others – for example, information about a customer's last purchase. Other data may be collected but not used by the business – in this case, you should consider whether or not this data is still needed going forward; don't collect and store data you don't need and are not going to utilise (don't forget to take note of how other teams are using this data so you don't get rid of something that is important to them!).

Once you have this information, then think about:

5. **What are you missing that you NEED to have?**

   What data do you not have that would be critical to fulfil your email marketing plans going forward – for example, additional purchase data?

6. **What are you missing that you'd LIKE to have?**

   What data do you not have that would be nice to have but not essential, to further enhance your email marketing plans going forward?

You will continue to build on the answers to these last two questions as you expand your email marketing plans.

7. **Why don't you currently have the information you need?**

   Is it because you're not collecting or tracking it? (Think about what tracking you currently have in place to support behavioural and purchase data and what additional tracking may be needed to extend the data you have available in the future.) Or is it because it's currently stored in a different system within your business and not currently accessible?

   The answers to this question will allow you to identify each of these problems and create a plan accordingly to either start collecting, or gain access to this data for future use.

In order to complete this part of the audit, you will definitely need input from other areas of the business, particularly your technology team who most likely control the database. Ask them to export a list of all the data fields you currently have stored to get you started.

When you know what you have and what's missing, you can start to fill these gaps – we'll talk about this in more detail as part of Chapter 2.

 **TAKE ACTION**

Answer the following questions to conduct your audit:

- What data do you currently have?
- Where is this data found within your business?
- Which pieces of this data are you currently using within your campaigns?
- Prioritise the data you have based on value to your company and email marketing programme.

List every data field individually so that you get a clear picture of everything that is available.

See Appendix 2 on page 298 for an example.

Then think about your future requirements:

- What are you missing that you NEED to have?
- What are you missing that you'd LIKE to have?
- Why don't you currently have this information?

You can download a copy of this as a worksheet here:
www.etelligencebook.com/members/step1/dataaudit/

CASE STUDY

Client Type: Hotel group (Lake District Hotels Ltd)

Objective: Increase direct bookings and reduce third-party commission whilst maintaining and increasing occupancy and revenue.

<u>Situation</u>

Founded in 1983, Lake District Hotels Ltd is a collection of unique family-owned hotels in the heart of the Lake District.

Lake District Hotels had disparate data sources with no integration between their general marketing and reservations database. This made it hard for them to understand their customers' lifetime value and send relevant, personalised campaigns.

They needed a single customer view to enable them to automate customer journeys with minimal time and resource.

Implementing Pure360's PureIntelligence module made this possible, and overall bookings increased by 4% in the first six months as a result.

Challenges

Like many hotel groups, Lake District Hotels Ltd had valuable guest information on legacy reservation systems with many incomplete or incorrect fields. For example, despite having a dog-friendly policy, they had no way of identifying if a visitor had brought their dog with them.

The reservations database was not integrated with their general marketing database, so they did not have a detailed understanding of their guests' journey and overall lifetime value.

Sending personalised, targeted campaigns based on customer lifecycle journeys and previous behaviour was almost impossible.

Cleaning the databases would have taken a significant amount of budget, time and resource that was not available at the time.

James Pass, Online Marketing Manager, explains, 'We wanted to be able to access our reservations data easily in order to target our previous guests in a much more efficient and personalised manner.'

In addition to email, Lake District Hotels Ltd also use direct mail as part of their overall mix. Like many marketing teams, they had issues with accurately attributing revenue and ROI per marketing channel.

The Solution

Lake District Hotels is a long-standing Pure360 customer, using PureCampaign to create and send their email campaigns.

Adding Pure360's PureIntelligence module was the natural solution to their data and personalisation challenges, as it offers a single customer view and automated customer journeys.

'We have used Pure360 for a few years and I thought PureIntelligence was the answer to our data management problems. Other solutions involved moving away from Pure360 and I didn't want to do that.'

The Pure360 team ensured Lake District Hotel Ltd's PureIntelligence on-boarding process ran smoothly, meeting all of the hotel group's specific needs.

1.3

Segmentation and Personalisation

Speak directly to different groups of subscribers on your list – they are not all the same.

Your email list consists of many different kinds of people, with different behaviour, profiles and interests.

Segmentation involves dividing up your email list into smaller groups that have commonalities in these areas, in order to provide them with more useful, relevant information, as opposed to sending the same information and offers to everyone.

This is the very definition of putting the customer at the heart of your email marketing strategy.

Segmentation is a tactic that every email marketer can and should be using, even if at a basic level. By narrowing your focus and breaking down your list into smaller, more targeted segments, you can devise content that speaks to these specific subscribers' needs and wants, providing information and offers that are more likely to engage them.

For example, a clothing retailer may create a segment of users on their list that are male, and another including female subscribers – each of these segments may receive different products, offers, wording and imagery based on that attribute.

Recipients are 75% more likely to click on emails from segmented campaigns than non-segmented campaigns; generating 14.64% more email opens and 59.99% more clicks.
(Source: MailChimp, 2017)[2]

As you become more advanced, you can start to layer up multiple attributes to create more complex and detailed segments, allowing you to create a better email strategy and content that aligns with the subscriber's wants and needs.

For example, you might decide to send a special offer for a new line of sandals to only female subscribers who, through data collected on sign-up or through a preference centre*, have registered an interest in receiving emails about casual shoe styles, have engaged with your email programme in the last three months and have made a previous purchase of shoes. In this way, you know the segment is more likely to engage with the content of your new email as it is highly relevant to active subscribers and will lead to a higher conversion rate.

The amount of segmentation you can do is only limited by the data you hold and the number of subscribers who meet that criterion (i.e. if the number is too small, is it worth the time to create the segment and corresponding content).

*A preference centre is a place where subscribers can alter their personal information and preferences relating to the email programme, for example.

In-Email Personalisation

Nearly half of consumers would be likely to engage more with retailers that send offers that are relevant and interesting to them.
(Source: Pure360)[3]

This tactic is effectively **1-2-1 segmentation** – sending targeted content, not to a group of subscribers in this case, but narrowing the focus further to provide information even more relevant to that specific subscriber.

For example, not only could you segment your database into groups of male and female and then tailor the main message and imagery accordingly, you could then use in-email personalisation to further target the specific products shown, based on that subscriber's previous purchases or recent website browse behaviour. So, each subscriber that received the email would see different product recommendations.

Personalising email content further increases relevancy and engagement rates, allowing you to provide a much better customer experience.

The technology you use and the data you hold will help you to personalise your content more effectively. The two main ways to do this are using:

- **Dynamic fields** – allowing data from fields in your database to be pulled directly into the email. For example, a subscriber's first name or the name of the product they have just purchased is added into the email copy.

  Always remember to have a contingency for when the field is not populated (for example, in the absence of first name, you could have an alternative default such as 'customer' or 'friend' or even leave this field blank).

- **Dynamic content** – this involves changing whole sections of your email, depending on the subscriber who is receiving the message, allowing different content to be sent to different subscribers without creating separate emails.

For example, showing a different header image or call-to-action wording, depending on whether the recipient is male or female.

This means that instead of creating and sending a separate email to each segment you have chosen, the majority of the content may be the same, but using this technique, you only need to build one email, and can still have differences in the content.

This works really well, particularly if you have a special message or offer to call out to one specific segment, for example, but the main content will be the same for everyone.

Nowadays this type of content includes real-time content, as we discussed as part of the contextual data pot – the ability to change content based on what is happening for the subscriber right now, such as the location they are in when opening the email.

But the difference here is that this type of dynamic content will change each time the email is opened, whereas standard dynamic content does not.

Both of these methods (group segmentation and in-email personalisation) can help you to send your email communications in a way that personalises them on a 1-2-1 basis – so that every email you send can be different and highly relevant to the person you are sending it to.

Within the five main groups of data we discussed in the last section, you should identify different fields in your database that can be used to highlight those commonalities between subscribers in your list for segmentation or for 1-2-1 personalisation.

These could include:

- **demographic information (gender, location etc.)** – for example, if you are advertising an event in London, segment the database to send an invite only to those living within 50 miles of the venue. Sending an invite to people outside of the UK would be deemed highly irrelevant.

- **interest data** – subscribers can inform preferences through a survey or preference centre, or purely through their behaviour with previous emails – what types of products/services/offers they click on and interact with. All of this information helps to create a picture of the users' interests, and the type of content they are more likely to respond to and be interested in.

- **previous purchaser behaviour** – for example, segmenting out non-purchasers who may need more nurturing and information vs. those who have already made a purchase from you. Insights on previous spend value, number of previous purchases, and time since the last purchase, can also help you to identify the most valuable subscribers and target them with different communications from those at the other end of the purchase path.

- **stage in the customer journey** – segmenting audiences based on their stage in the customer journey (discussed further in Chapters 2 and 3) is one of the most valuable ways to customise your emails. For example:

  o Welcome new subscribers with more generalised information about your brand, products and services, and the benefits you offer (for example, a welcome email and on-boarding series) to help build a relationship.

  o Pique the interest of those who have been on your email list for a longer period of time with communications giving them different options, more product/service-specific information etc.

o   Nurture those who are at risk of exiting without purchasing with an abandoned cart message to bring them back in.

- **email activity** – based on email open and click data, identify active (those who are currently engaging with your campaigns), passive (those who have engaged in the recent past), and inactive subscribers (those who haven't engaged for a while) to be more focused with your targeting. You could also look at specific emails a subscriber has opened and links clicked relating to distinct products or information, to show you what they are most interested in and allow you to target them accordingly.

- **website behaviour** – by tracking a user's behaviour on a website (pages browsed, when they last logged in to their account, searches carried out, icons clicked, videos watched etc.), targeted emails based on this activity can be sent. Many of these emails can also be automated to ensure the right message is being sent to the right person at the right time to garner the best response.

 TAKE ACTION

How are you using the data that you currently have to segment and personalise your emails at the moment?

When reviewing your current strategy, consider who you are sending your emails to and whether the content is relevant to that person.

- Review your current segmentation strategy (if you are currently using any segmentation in your campaigns). Based on the data you currently have, make a note of what segments you:

  o regularly use in your campaigns
  o sometimes use in your campaigns
  o have available but rarely/never use in your campaigns
  o would like to create and start using in your campaigns for increased targeting and relevancy

- Conduct a SWOT analysis of your segmentation strategy.

A SWOT analysis allows you to evaluate the effectiveness of your current strategy across its Strengths, Weaknesses, Opportunities and Threats (see an example on next page).

STRENGTHS	WEAKNESSES
Characteristics of the current segmentation strategy that give it an advantage	*Characteristics of the current segmentation strategy that place the business at a disadvantage*
For example: • Simple and enables fast data selections • Targets most of the prospects and customers that have a higher propensity to purchase	For example: • Current strategy does not consider customer loyalty and frequency over time, beyond the last interaction/sale • There is no separation between purchase behaviour and email behaviour
OPPORTUNITIES	**THREATS**
Elements in the environment that the business or project could exploit to its advantage	*Elements in the environment that could cause trouble for the business or project*
For example: • Include email behaviour in segmentation • Implement additional segments around purchase frequency and value to better target customers with offers and information	For example: • Sophisticated segmentation of competitors resulting in more niche targeting and higher relevance

- Using the data list in the table you created in the last task, make a note next to each of the data you use:

  o to create segments
  o as dynamic fields within your email content
  o for dynamic content purposes

- Review how you are currently personalising your emails:

  o How often do you personalise your campaigns with this information?

o Do you personalise your email content in any of your emails? Note down which email types you often do this for against each of the following:

- browse behaviour
- previous purchase behaviour
- email open/click behaviour

You can download a copy of this as a worksheet here:
www.etelligencebook.com/members/step1/segmentation/

1.4
Automated Campaign Strategy

Automated emails generate 320% more revenue than non-automated emails.
(Source: Campaign Monitor)[4]

But they meet the basic marketing need:

Sending the right message, to the right person, at the right time.

I've already talked about segmentation and personalisation in the last section – *sending the right message to the right person.*

Automated campaigns (aka autoresponders/triggered emails) meet that third need – *sending at the right time.*

They are the backbone of a successful email marketing strategy and are critical to allow you to create a programme that truly connects with your subscribers at the right time. These emails are set up within your ESP and send automatically based on specific trigger rules.

Types of Automated Campaign

When reviewing what you currently have in place, I want you to keep in mind the three main types of automated campaigns to include in your email marketing strategy:

1. **Transactional emails** – these are messages triggered by a purchase.

    For example, confirming order details and delivery date, or order shipped notifications. These types of campaign deliver specific information about a purchase, your account, vital service messages or statutory legal notices, and are generally not used for marketing purposes.

2. **Lead-nurturing emails** – this is the practice of building relationships with prospects even when they are not currently looking to buy a product or service.

    The aim of lead-nurturing is to place your business front-of-mind for the prospect, so that they will be more likely to place an order with you when they are ready to do so.

    Lead-nurturing may be as basic as an occasional email providing updates about a product/service, or relevant helpful information (for example, a monthly newsletter or a specific product-focused sales email), through to a more directed series of emails to 'educate' the prospect and lead them through the buying process.

3. **Behaviour-based emails** – when a subscriber takes an action (or doesn't), an email (or series of emails) is triggered. An action could include engagement with email campaigns, purchase history, or even actions taken (or not) on a website.

    For example, if a subscriber adds items to their online shopping basket and does not go on to complete the purchase, a series of emails could be triggered at 2, 24 and 72 hours after this has happened to encourage them back to complete the order.

We'll go into more detail about different types of campaigns within each of these at different stages of the customer journey, and best practice recommendations in Chapters 2 and 3.

Over the years, I've worked with an array of different companies at varying stages of implementation of their automated campaign strategy. Some had nothing in place at all and others had a wide selection of campaigns targeting different stages of the customer journey already up and running.

Wherever you currently are with your strategy, as with every element we are reviewing in this chapter, it's important to have a clear view of what is currently in place for your business and WHY it's in place – when does it target the customer/prospect?

This is especially important with automations as they are not looked at every day in the same way as manual campaigns are. They may contain out-of-date or broken data or functionality that needs to be fixed and so should be reviewed regularly (not just as part of an overall audit).

Remember, not all automations will be triggered through your ESP. Don't forget to look at your internal systems, CRM and eCommerce platforms to ensure you cover all emails that a subscriber may receive under any circumstances. Even if you're not responsible for them, you should know that they are there and are part of the overall communications strategy that your subscribers see.

When creating automations, you should also consider their place within your overall email programme – this will include any exclusions (subscribers who are not eligible to receive the email for various reasons such as having purchased in the last 30 days) and the priority order of the automation (if another automation is running or manual email being sent, which is more important for them to receive and therefore takes priority to be sent?).

Because automations run independently of your manual campaign schedule, it's important to consider these elements to make sure that your subscribers don't receive more emails than you want them to within a specific time period (for example, per day or per week), as well as ensuring that the campaigns most likely to prompt a conversion are prioritised. For example, abandoned basket emails are more likely to encourage a purchase than a general promotional email because they target an action the subscriber has already started to take.

✎ TAKE ACTION

Thinking about the three main types of automated campaigns, add to the current strategy outline you started creating (page 26) and ensure you list all of your current automations – include all those you have running at the moment, as well as those that exist but are not currently live (note why they were turned off if this is the case).

See Appendix 3 on page 300 for three examples of common automated campaigns you may already find in your business.

Also consider additional information such as any exclusions in place and the priority order of the automation.

For all those you've listed, get a copy of every email in each series, and then evaluate the following additional areas:

Set-up

- Is any regular, documented testing conducted?

- Do you have reporting available? If so, gather these stats together and look for trends over time in each campaign's performance.

- Are the triggers correct and working properly?

- Are the exclusions in place the right ones? For example, should people who have purchased in the last 30 days still receive an abandoned basket email?

<u>Design</u>

- Does it match your company branding? Is it mobile responsive? Is it clear and actionable? What do you like/dislike about the current design? Does it encourage conversion?

- Content – is it up-to-date? Is it accurate? Is it in your brand tone? Does it include information that would make you want to take an action to fulfil the goal of the campaign?

- Do you have the ability to make changes to the template?

You can download a copy of this as a worksheet here:
www.etelligencebook.com/members/step1/automatedcampaigns/

1.5

Design

The design of your emails plays a big part in helping or hindering how subscribers interact with the content you are sending to them.

It's important to ensure your design encourages subscribers through to your main call-to-action and, most importantly, doesn't confuse them or give them too many options in one go.

Your email should be like a shop window – a gateway to more information.

In this stage of the process, I want you to consider how you and your team currently feel about your emails – try and take a step back and be really objective – as well as using data to back up your opinions. You need to ascertain what's working and what's not currently working for you so that you can take steps to improve.

Also, there are a range of myths that people believe about email design that you need to ensure that you're not fooled by. These include:

1. **'Long emails are bad'**

   In general, this myth is actually true – you don't want to give people too many options within an email.

   But some businesses do buck this trend on some occasions – such as some B2B businesses that deliver an entire blog post within the email (where they don't have the goal of driving someone back to their website to make a purchase, for example, but simply want them to read the information).

The key here is to test what is right for YOUR business, audience and email type – test to find the optimum email length for you and the purpose of your email.

2. **'You can only use standard system fonts in your designs'**

Although in most cases standard system fonts are the main ones available and will always be your backup in any case, web fonts are starting to become more widely used, with online font repositories starting to cover email use in their licensing (such as Google Fonts – one of the most popular and easy to use sources of web fonts).

Fonts such as Arial, Verdana, Georgia, Times New Roman and Courier are considered standard fonts that can be used for text in email design. They're the default fonts that are found on different computers, devices and operating systems, and exist on almost all devices.

Web fonts aren't typically found in multiple operating systems and devices – web font support depends on the email client and how the web font is embedded in the email. But where they are supported, it means that any web fonts used in your branding can also be used in your email design, making the experience more cohesive for the subscriber.

Generally, the following email clients have good support for web fonts:

o   Apple Mail
o   Android (default mail client, not Gmail app)
o   iOS Mail
o   Outlook 2000
o   Outlook.com app
o   Thunderbird

3. 'You can't use animated or background images in email'

Similarly to web fonts, depending on how you code the background images into your email, there can be limited support for them in different email clients. So, although they can be used, you should ensure that your main information is not contained in them and that they back up your design rather than being a main factor.

When it comes to animated GIFs (images that display a series of pictures to produce the illusion of motion), these can be a fantastic way to illustrate different details within your email and bring an element of 'life' into your design as well as highlight/support important information.

The key to using an animated GIF in your email design is to ensure that their inclusion in the email is to support your content so that even without the animation (in the small number of places that these are now not supported), the email still displays in a way that is eye catching and encourages conversion.

As a backup, you should ensure that if the animation doesn't work, the first frame of the GIF contains your most important information (such as a call-to-action, offer, or headline). Note that Outlook 2007, 2010 and 2013 won't show the animation; instead, they will show the first frame.

4. 'You only need one call-to-action'

Yes, you should definitely focus on one KEY call-to-action in your email to ensure that you don't confuse readers with lots of different actions, but to encourage the action you desire, you should ensure you repeat your call-to-action **at least** 2/3 times throughout your email.

This should be done through the use of text links, images and 'bullet-proof' buttons (buttons that show and can be clicked on even when images are disabled – they are built into the HTML code of your email design to look like 'image' buttons, for example, with rounded corners).

5. **'I can create an email that is made up entirely of images'**

Although this is technically possible, it's not something I would recommend doing.

Images are still disabled by default in some email clients (such as many versions of Outlook) and if your emails are completely made up of images, the viewing experience for the subscriber will be broken and your message illegible when images don't show.

With the increase in mobile devices, you may want to consider slightly altered designs for different devices where images are more supported – such as iOS devices where images are turned on by default.

Generally, for desktop and webmail versions of your email, it is prudent to design your emails with image blocking in mind, including plenty of text and bullet-proof buttons. This means that even with images turned off, the main message and call-to-action of the email can still be seen and acted upon.

6. **'Your email design should look exactly the same across different devices'**

There are now many different types of device that your subscribers are opening and reading their emails on, making it necessary to have a slightly different design for each.

The screen size alone on many of these devices means that how people interact with your emails will differ. Not only that, the technology available on different devices will allow you more flexibility in some cases (such as the use of web fonts on iOS devices for example).

You should always think about how you can optimise your email design for maximum engagement on different devices, including removing or stacking elements of your email. This can involve having certain sections that don't show on mobile devices, or stacking a two-column design into one column on a mobile device to ensure that the information and call-to-action is accessible on a smaller screen without pinching and scrolling. Another feature you can use is a hamburger menu where your menu stacks and can be accessed by clicking on a button – it looks something like this on your screen: ≡

What is Your Design Process?

With different departments involved, different email types and branding considerations in play, this is often an area that causes a lot of tension within businesses and can take up a lot of time.

How long does it currently take for you to create a new email campaign?

For some businesses, the whole processes of briefing, creation, testing, QA (quality assurance process) and eventual approval can take a couple of weeks! Are you in this situation?

What if you could speed up your design process? What would this mean to your business? Would it mean the ability to save resources and maybe even send more emails, quicker and with better content, generating more revenue for your business?

By analysing your design process as well as the technology and resources (internal or external) that you use to support you, you can easily achieve these benefits.

 # TAKE ACTION

Gather a selection of emails sent by your company over the last six months (including at least two of each email type you send – for example, newsletters vs. departmental sales emails vs. automations etc.) and their send results.

TIP: *Printing them out so that you can write on them and see them as a whole may be helpful, as well as looking at them on screen to see which elements appear after each scroll.*

- Critically analyse each of the emails you've gathered:
  - o What do you like about these emails?
  - o What don't you like about these emails?

Pay close attention to the different elements such as subject lines (does the subject line reflect the email content?), length, copy, call-to-action, design, imagery etc.

- Take a look at the data associated with each of these emails – which was the best performing and which was the worst performing?

Why do you think this was?

Look at not only your normal metrics, but if you have the ability to in your sending platform, look at click heatmaps to ascertain where subscribers clicked within the email (an image representation of which links were clicked in your email).

Also think about:

- What set templates do you currently have that are used for different email types (if any)?

o Do you have a modular template design that can be used across different email types? (Modular email templates consist of separate sections or modules which can be changed, rearranged, removed or customised, as opposed to a set design whose format cannot be changed other than to switch out copy or images in set places within the design.)

o What do you like and dislike about your current templates? For example, when creating new emails, are they easy to use and change sections? Do you have the flexibility you'd like?

- Is your email design consistent with your company branding? Does your brand come across clearly in all emails, across different email types?

- Do you distinguish between different email types within your designs?

- Is your call-to-action clear and accessible?

You can download a copy of this as a worksheet here: www.etelligencebook.com/members/step1/design/

Email Design Process

- Get yourself a range of Post-it notes in different colours and a blank wall, then map out on the wall your current design process:

o What is your current design process? Use a different colour of Post-it notes for each stage of the process – for example, briefing, design, copywriting, approval – and create a flow of what happens each time an email is created and sent.

o Note the people that are involved at each stage of the process, the tasks that happen, the time this usually takes and any other details to note for each stage.

- Then looking at your current flow, think about where you could streamline the process:

  o Are there more people involved in each stage than needed?

  o Do you have complete control over how your templates are created at the moment or is each created individually (taking up more time and resources)? Could these be more templated for better brand consistency and efficiency?

  o Is there a way to speed up the testing and QA processes?

  o Are you setting deadlines at the point of briefing that include time for revisions and testing?

  o Does your current technology support the process or is there any other technology you could bring in to help you better manage the process?

1.6
Results Tracking

Now that we know what you're sending, to whom and when, let's take a closer look at your results.

On an ongoing basis, you should be keeping a record of each send you do and its associated statistics. When it comes to analysing your campaigns, depending on your business, you will have a plethora of numbers to look at. These may include standard metrics such as:

Deliverability Metrics

These statistics are a measure of how many emails were delivered to recipients (not the number that reached the inbox – we discuss the difference in Chapter 5) and include:

- sent number (the number of emails that leave your email system)
- bounces
  These are split into two categories:
  o hard bounces: email addresses that do not exist
  o soft bounces: email addresses that produce a temporary failure to deliver, such as mailbox full
- delivered number (and % rate)
  This is calculated using the two numbers above:

Number of emails sent MINUS Bounces

Positive Engagement Metrics

These are metrics that indicate a positive action has been taken by the recipient:

- Open number (and % rate) (total and unique)

Number of opens ÷ number delivered
(x 100 for a percentage rate)

- Click rate (and % rate) (total and unique)

Number of clicks ÷ number delivered
(x 100 for a percentage rate)

- CTOR (click-to-open rate)

Number of clicks ÷ number of opens
(x 100 for a percentage rate)

If applicable and available in your business, here you may also be tracking and recording values such as:

- number of transactions (orders)

- conversion rate (conversions could be transactions, but could also be downloads, video views or any other action you want the subscriber to take after clicking on your email)

Number of conversions ÷ number of emails delivered
(x 100 for a percentage rate)

- total revenue generated

- revenue per email

   Total revenue ÷ number of emails delivered
   (x 100 for a percentage rate)

- AOV (average order value)

   Total revenue ÷ number of orders

Negative Engagement Metrics

These are metrics that indicate a negative action has been taken by the recipient:

- Complaint number (and % rate)

   Number of complaints ÷ number delivered
   (x 100 for a percentage rate)

- Unsubscribe number (and % rate)

   Number of unsubscribes ÷ number delivered
   (x 100 for a percentage rate)

Don't forget to also keep a track of your website metrics which can be really useful when analysing, not just website performance, but email performance too! Using programmes such as Google Analytics, you can access a wealth of additional information about your landing page performance including:

- bounce rate
- exit rate
- time on page
- conversion rate
- action rates – such as video plays and downloads

If you are using a landing page specifically for an email campaign, record these alongside your campaign metrics taken from your ESP, as well as generally keeping a record of key statistics for your website.

The landing page you are driving subscribers to when clicking on your call-to-action is critical to ensure the journey is fluid and a conversion is made as easily as possible.

Analysing Your Results for Trends

You should not only be looking at individual email and campaign series results, but also to analyse these results for trends in different areas such as:

- **over time** – do your results increase or decrease over a period of time?

- **per campaign type** (for example, newsletters vs. promotional emails vs. automations) – which is your best and worst performing campaign type? Which generates the most and least revenue for you (if this is your goal)?

- **per campaign** (for example, abandoned basket campaign vs. abandoned browse vs. welcome on-boarding series) – which sees the highest positive engagement?

- **by offer type** – which offer type generates the most engagement? For example, 10% off vs. 40% off or % off vs. £ off.

- **by time of year** – do your email results reflect the normal trends within your business?

There are a multitude of ways in which you can analyse your campaigns, and these are just a few.

As well as looking for overall trends, don't forget to look for differences between subject line types (length, sentiment, style etc.) and elements within your campaigns such as call-to-action wording or colour, email design and anything else you can distinguish between. This will become especially prominent when testing.

Additionally, be sure to review the results of each email and series of emails as a whole against your business and email marketing goals, and adjust regularly to maximise results. For example, if you see that one email is performing much lower than others within an automated series of emails, you may want to test different content; in this case, though, it is important to remember that it is common to see a decrease in results as subscribers move through a series and drop off at certain points.

Most importantly, ensure you look at not only individual statistics but also a combination of statistics to see the true performance of your campaigns. For example, if the goal of an email is just to have the subscriber open and read the content, looking just at the open rate is a good indicator of its effectiveness. However, if the goal is for them to click through and take a next action, just looking at the open rate is not going to tell you if that email has performed to its best ability.

✎ TAKE ACTION

Take note of the following information relating to how you track and measure your email marketing:

- What statistics are you currently tracking for each email campaign you send out?

  o What do you have available in your ESP?

  o What additional statistics do you track (for example, conversion rate or other website analytics)?

  o What statistics are not currently available in each of these areas that you would like to see?

- How regularly do you analyse your results and look for trends?

You can download a copy of this as a worksheet here:
www.etelligencebook.com/members/step1/results/

Then...

- Take a look at your last 6–12 months' worth of campaign data (including all metrics available to you).

  Using a spreadsheet (and pivot tables if you are proficient in using them), analyse for trends. For example, are open/click rates increasing/decreasing? Are complaint rates increasing? Is this trend overall or just for specific email types?

1.7
Testing Strategy

Implementing a well-documented and ongoing testing strategy into your business can provide both quick and big wins!

Testing is important in order to continuously learn and inform your overall strategy, content development, image selection and design, and improve your campaign results.

Even a small uplift in open or click-through volumes can often make a big impact on conversions, sales, and revenue.

The key is to test one element (or combination) at a time to always know which change has instigated a difference in results and review the metric that is most appropriate to the element under consideration.

What Elements of Your Emails Can You Test?

There are an almost unlimited number of elements within your email marketing that you can test.

Some of these include:

- **Email subject line** – you could test different subject lines to see which techniques and styles garner the highest results. Although many people only look at open rate when testing the subject line, it is also important to consider other deeper metrics such as conversion rates in the final result analysis if the goal of your email isn't to get it opened, but to move people through to an action. For example, a more specific subject line may produce a slightly lower open rate (as only the people truly interested will open it) but will produce a higher click and conversion rate since those opening are more engaged with the content once inside the email.

- **The offer given** – think about whether a 10% discount or £50 off works best. Are secondary offers useful in elevating overall response rates? Try and ascertain the offer amount and style that has the most impact with your audience.

- **Broadcast timing** – test sending emails at different times of the day/ days of the week for maximum impact. You may also want to trial using 'send time optimisation' (available in some ESPs and other third-party systems) to optimise the send time to each individual subscriber's behaviour, rather than one send time for the whole list.

- **Tone of voice** – trial using a formal vs. a conversational tone in email copy, for example.

- **Copy length** – for example, try long vs. short copy or whether this is displayed broken down into three sections, or six sections.

- **Your CTA (call-to-action)** – test the number and location of links, as well as the wording used, colour, and size of buttons.

- **Personalisation** – identify what is the most effective form of personalisation for different targeting approaches and dynamic messaging.

- **Frequency interval for email marketing** – assess how to achieve the balance between over- and under-emailing as well as maximising revenue.

- **Touch strategy for triggered emails (automated campaigns)** – trial which sequence of offers and intervals works best.

- **Segmentation approaches** – trial delivering messages with a particular offer, imagery or other content specific to those subscribers.

How Are You Testing?

There are two main ways to run tests on your email marketing campaigns:

1. **A/B split testing**

    Simple A/B tests are where one type of content is tested head-to-head against another, splitting the test list into equal sections.

    For example, one subject line type tested against another, or against multiple different versions (A vs. B / A vs. B vs. C vs. D etc.), but all with the same element tested.

    There are two types of A/B testing:

    o **Partial-testing** – this usually takes the form of a trial email sent to a sub-set of your target audience, with different campaign elements. This test is despatched prior to the roll-out, to enable the main campaign to feature the optimum combination of variables.

       For example, to establish which of two different subject lines works the best, email two 'cells', each comprising 10% of the whole list. The cell that achieves the highest results is the 'winner', and this subject line can then be rolled out to the remaining 80% of the database.

A test cell should be taken randomly from the wider list; for example, don't just take the first 5,000 records in a list as this will often select only the longest serving subscribers.

Your test cell should be smaller than the main list, but large enough for the differences in response to be statistically significant; i.e. it is unlikely to have occurred by chance.

o **Live testing** – in this approach, different creative treatments are tested during the full campaign, in order to change the creative approach later in the same campaign or for future campaigns.

For example, one half of your list would receive one subject line, and the other would receive a different subject line. The send that achieves the highest positive engagement identifies the subject line that is most effective.

2. Multivariate testing

Multivariate testing involves testing a range of variables (rather than just variations of one element as in A/B testing) in order to find the optimum combination of variants.

You select different elements of the email and create a number of variations of these individual elements which are then combined to create different versions of the email.

For example, if you were running a test on two elements of your email (the headline and the call-to-action copy for example) with three differing versions of each (one control version in your usual style and two variation versions), you would have nine unique combinations which would then be tested against each other to determine the winner:

Headline 1 Call-To-Action 1	Headline 2 Call-To-Action 1	Headline 3 Call-To-Action 1
Headline 1 Call-To-Action 2	Headline 2 Call-To-Action 2	Headline 3 Call-To-Action 2
Headline 1 Call-To-Action 3	Headline 2 Call-To-Action 3	Headline 3 Call-To-Action 3

Multivariate testing is a much more advanced and comprehensive way to test different email elements.

There is no limit as to the number of variables you can test – the goal of multivariate testing is to determine which combination of variations performs the best out of all the possible combinations.

For example, to test three different calls-to-action, three different headlines and three different images, will create 27 versions of the campaign, and your list will need to be split between this many cells.

If your list is relatively small, you may not have enough data to create a statistically significant result; therefore, start off with a small number of options to keep the number of combinations low.

Your Testing Strategy

It is important to document any testing you do on your campaigns.

Think about any testing you've already done and record the results of these so that they can be used going forward.

Many clients that I work with fall into the common trap of running individual tests on one campaign – for example, 'I think that this subject line will generate more opens than this subject line'. In 99% of cases, this type of testing won't produce a significant result that will allow you to learn anything specific that can be carried forward to other campaigns, because the test was 'in the moment'.

In order to create a testing plan that has a significant impact on your email marketing programme, it's important to know WHY you are testing an element and WHAT makes a winning result.

I'll break this down in more detail in Chapter 2 and I'll show you **my 5-step process to running meaningful tests.**

✎ TAKE ACTION

- Think about the following elements in relation to your current testing strategy:

  o What tests, if any, are you currently running?

  o Are you testing regularly or sporadically?

  o Are you recording the results of each test in order to use this information to inform future campaigns?

  o Do you know WHY you are running each test and what you expect to achieve?

  o How do you currently determine a winner and a learning to take forward from each test?

- Make sure you have recorded the details of any tests you have recently conducted in a spreadsheet.

You can download your split test planning kit here:
www.etelligencebook.com/members/step1/testing/

1.8

Technology and Processes

As the final part of your audit, you need to take a look at the technology you're using and the processes and resources you have in place to run your campaigns.

According to the Direct Marketing Association's Marketer Email Tracker 2018, some of the most significant challenges to successfully executing an email marketing programme include inefficient internal processes and outdated ESP technology.

The Technology You're Using

When evaluating the technology you are using to manage your data and execute your send strategy, it is important to consider not only your current requirements, but also what you would like to be implementing in 6, 12 and 24 months' time, in order to find a system that allows your programme to grow and improve.

To manage their email marketing campaigns, businesses have traditionally used software that focuses purely on email marketing, traditionally known by email marketers as Email Service Providers or ESPs.

However, the name 'ESP' is probably a bit misleading nowadays since most now offer far more than just the management of email campaigns. Instead, they are platforms for managing communications across the whole customer relationship, from when a prospect first subscribes via a landing page to when customers purchase, including multiple opportunities to send personalised emails and integrate with social media platforms, for example.

So, it's important to decide what type of system is right for your business – an email-only ESP platform, or one which encompasses other channels as well – likely a marketing automation platform.

Your Email Development Process

It's important to have a clearly documented process plan within your organisation. With movements in staff members, without a clear strategy and process plan in place, your programme's direction can be negatively impacted.

It takes time for new members of staff to learn processes and procedures, and problems with your programme, such as campaigns not running as they should (automations not firing/duplicates being sent), incorrect content in campaigns and negative engagement or deliverability trends, can easily go unnoticed.

Getting your email processes in place and optimised isn't sexy – but it's necessary.

Before you jump into 'the next big idea' or implementing a shiny new system or the next email trend, think about your current processes. If you could improve them and save time whilst ensuring accuracy, think about all that extra time that you COULD then spend on new and exciting projects... so, start here and don't skip this step in your email audit.

We touched on this briefly regarding email design, but that's only one part of the process – your full email development process will contain the following steps:

- **Planning**
  This includes what you will send, when, why and how.

  When creating your email marketing strategy, you will most likely need to include different departments' input, branding considerations, seasonal campaigns, planned sales and other information.

  Consider who needs to be involved at this stage to help you create and approve your plans, as well as ensuring that they meet the wider needs of the organisation and its overarching goals.

  Most importantly, don't forget to put the needs of the customer first in all your plans to produce the highest results.

- **Production**
  This section involves elements including the creation of:
  o your email design
  o copywriting
  o imagery
  o landing page development
  o creative build in your ESP
  o quality assurance process

  ... everything that is required to get your email ready to send.

  This is likely to be the part of the process that involves the most people. Briefs will also need to be created to gather each section together – for example, a brief for your designers to document what you would like within your email layout and imagery.

- **Broadcast**
  When you're about to press the 'send' button, there are two main elements to consider:

o Targeting – what segmentation and personalisation are you using to ensure your campaign is highly relevant? This will need to be set up to pull in the right data for your broadcast.

o Split testing – are you running any testing on your email that needs to be set up and recorded?

- **Analysis**
  Once the email has sent, it's important to go back over what happened, and record and analyse your performance statistics, including your email analytics and website statistics.

  Don't forget to also sign up for your own email programme so that you can experience it as a subscriber would! It's important to review what you're doing from an external perspective, as well as your internal analysis.

Your Quality Assurance Process

Marketers spend on average 3.9 hours having an email reviewed and securing approval – more time than they spend on email copywriting, design, development, or any other component of email production.
(Source: State of Email Workflows – Litmus)[5]

All emails should go through a quality assurance (QA) process before being broadcast; this is a crucial step that must not be left out of your email production process to ensure sends are mistake-free. Your QA process not only needs to test and produce error-free emails, but do it as quickly as possible.

Your QA process should include the following elements:

- Reviewing email content – copy, imagery, offers, key details. And don't forget your 'from' name and subject line too!
- Spelling and grammar checks
- Email rendering – does your email render well in all email clients that are the most used by your subscribers? Does your email get clipped in Gmail?
- Validating links (and ensuring they not only work but go to the correct landing page)
- Checking imagery – that the right images have been used, alt text is present, sizes are optimised for email size and load time and that with images disabled, the image is still actionable and the main message can be seen
- Ensuring tracking works properly
- Testing your email's load time
- Spam testing – check your emails across key spam filters to identify and resolve issues before you send
- Checking branding and design guidelines have been followed
- Ensuring plain text version has been created
- Checking HTML code is valid
- Testing that the unsubscribe link is functional
- Data checks – are the right data fields being pulled through? Is there data in those fields within the database?
- Send data/segmentation – is the appropriate audience being targeted for the send? Has the right data/segment been selected for the send?
- Automations – have the right emails been added into the sequence at the right time?
- Dynamic content logic – has a backup been put in place in the event that a recipient doesn't meet the logic options specified?

You can download a copy of this as a checklist here:
www.etelligencebook.com/members/step1/technology/

You may also use external third-party systems to test email rendering etc., allowing you to save time in parts of this process, as opposed to conducting this testing manually.

Having someone else QA your work is of course best practice – but we don't always have that luxury. If you're on your own, make time where you can dedicate your full attention to performing the QA process and go through your checklist one by one.

TAKE ACTION

The Technology You're Using

Think about the following:

- What's your current situation?

  o What software are you using now?

    Think about not only your ESP/marketing automation platform but also any third-party providers such as deliverability tracking, real-time content, or Artificial Intelligence platforms.

  o Have you outgrown your current platform?

    Switching platforms is often due to either unmet customer service expectations or having outgrown your current platform – your marketing strategy is evolving and you need a platform that does more.

    So, it's important to ensure your new platform solves these current pain points and supports you in moving your strategy forward.

    Think about your current, imminent and future needs – do your current platforms have any areas that aren't accounted for?

    Is it possible to find a third-party to 'plug in' and provide this functionality or would you need to investigate a new sending platform altogether?

o What are your short, medium and long-term goals?

You need to know upfront what your goals for your email marketing are and therefore, for your new platform. Bring key stakeholders in your organisation together to ascertain your goals.

For example, do you want to:

- improve the speed with which leads move through the customer journey
- optimise the customer experience through the addition of more campaigns
- boost revenue by increasing conversion at key stages in the customer journey
- ensure your campaigns are optimised for mobile users
- integrate SMS to reach subscribers through a different channel as part of a more integrated strategy
- automate more of your campaigns for increased relevancy and targeting

• Create a list of your five biggest problems with your current ESP and the five things you love, to help you outline your needs.

Biggest problems with our current platform	Things we love about our current platform

- Determine your future ESP/marketing automation platform requirements.

  Consider your future technology needs across the following areas:

  o Integration with other systems
  o Functionality to allow you to implement specific email marketing tactics (such as segmentation or dynamic content capabilities)
  o Usability – how easy it is to navigate
  o Budget and resources you have available to implement a new system

- Complete the grid below to get clear on your priorities:

  o Get crystal clear on the features that are critical to your strategy, those that have a medium importance, and those that you would like to have but could live without.
  o Colour code your features – green if you have that feature in your current provider, and red if not.

Priority	Feature	Notes
Critical	 • • •	
Medium importance	 • • •	
Non-critical but nice to have	 • • •	

You can download a copy of this as a worksheet here:
www.etelligencebook.com/members/step1/technology

Your Email Development Process

With a blank wall and different coloured Post-it notes, map out your email development process.

- Detail every stage of the process including:

    o the stage in the process
    o what the task is that is being conducted
    o who is responsible for completing the task (department and person)
    o any systems that are used
    o any review stages throughout the process

- Then look at this process objectively – where could you cut out unnecessary tasks/people's involvement? For example, if your email creative is being reviewed by five people before you are able to take it into production, three of whom are on the same team, can this be streamlined to one person who gives overall feedback and approval rather than waiting for a response from all three?

    Where could time be saved?

    Where could there be areas of weakness that could allow for errors to occur?

By physically sticking Post-it notes to the wall to document this, you have a visual representation of your process that can be physically moved around to find the optimal flow.

Don't forget to take pictures and document the process before you remove it from the wall!

CASE STUDY

Client Type: Radio – Global Radio (home to some of the UK's best-loved radio stations such as Heart, Capital and Classic FM)

Objective: To simplify and speed up the email creation process.

Situation
Many of the Global Radio brands – Heart is a good example – operate locally across the UK. Heart has 22 stations, so we've been able to send national campaigns that also include content tailored for the recipient's local area. We also curate content based on things like engagement and previous activity. Being able to manage the content required for this in Taxi has helped us get more from our sending platform.

Challenges
Before Kim Doan, Head of CRM, joined at Global, email had been created manually. There were many templates in use, and often any updates we wanted to make had to be made at code level.

It took a long time to create email campaigns, which was a challenge as news in the entertainment industry changes often. We'd have to change content half way through creating an email, in order to stay up-to-date by the time we send.

This manual process was not only time-consuming, it was also costly.

After I joined, we went through a process to move to one central ESP, but before then, email was made in various systems, often using editor tools that were difficult to use and sometimes weren't even supported anymore!

The Solution
What does the email creation process look like now?
Now it's really easy for our team to create email. We have a set of master templates – one per brand – which have everything we need and are easy to maintain. The CRM lead for each brand is responsible for putting the layout and content together in Taxi, but they work collaboratively with editors and bloggers who know the content in depth.

Being able to add content straight into the email means it's quicker for us to make – this ensures content is fresher, and means we don't need to go into the HTML on a daily basis. We have a connector with Sailthru, our ESP, so once we're ready, we can export to there, assign an audience and hit the send button.

We create content for all of our brands using Taxi, so controls around permission and workflow are important. We can ensure that the content for the right brand is exported to the right instance of Sailthru.

On average, how long does it take to create email campaigns using Taxi?
It's helped us increase productivity significantly; I'd say we've reduced creation time and effort by about 80%. A good indicator of this is when we host events like the Summertime Ball. Now we

use Taxi, we can get all the content together from the party, and send the wrap-up email on the same day as people go home.

What reaction did the team have to the new process?
The team is a lot happier now – they're still busy, but they get a lot of work done. They're more empowered to try out new ideas, and strive to make the best we can.

Which KPIs has Taxi helped you improve?
We've been able to create more email campaigns – aside from regular newsletter-type content, we also send commercial and partner emails.

Being able to make these easily has meant we can send more, and this has helped us generate a lot more revenue from the email channel.

In addition, we built more in-depth tracking into our templates in Taxi, so we have also been able to prove the value of email a lot more than we had before.

What does the future hold for email marketing at Global Radio?
Now that we have the day-to-day nailed, we have more time to look at pushing the boundaries with our campaigns. We're looking at adding some more creative flair to some key campaigns, particularly for some of our big events.

CHAPTER 2

IMPROVE
What You're Doing

The #1 way you can take control of your email marketing and start making a difference to your results TODAY...

optimise what you're already doing!

Now that you have a clear idea of where you are right now, it's time to start improving what you already have!

In this chapter, we will go through each of the eight key sections again, this time looking at what you could do differently to improve your current results.

This involves enhancing, tweaking and adding to what you already have – we will look at adding new campaigns in Chapter 3.

2.1

Send Strategy

Content is an integral part of your email marketing send strategy and the first place to start when it comes to optimising what you already have in place to maximise your impact.

Having a documented strategy for what you want to send (particularly automated campaigns) and a content calendar to track when you're sending manual campaigns, helps map out every piece of communication over time. You created a record of both of these in the task in Chapter 1.

Having this clear view of your communications means you can make sure that each email works together to provide cohesive value and content, as well as supporting your wider marketing strategy and achievement of business objectives.

You can see what you already have planned (if anything), how these campaigns fit together and how they will work to keep customers engaging with your programme. It will also allow you to ascertain what resources you need over the next year to fulfil this strategy, for example, design and copywriting resources.

So, the next step is to analyse all of the information you've pulled together so far and identify any gaps in the content you're currently sending. Think about how this could be improved to better serve who your audience are (segmentation), their needs (dynamic content) and the situation they are in right now (automated campaigns).

To optimise the content you're currently sending, consider creating content buckets to prevent lethargy (different types of content that you roll out across different campaigns and emails at different times). You can also create an element of transparency within your email plans, in order to keep subscriber interest as high as possible. This could include having:

- overarching monthly themes
- specific email themes
- month start/end newsletters

This could also include rotating between blog posts, videos, featured categories of products, behind the scenes info and specific product focuses, for example, to keep subscribers interested and opening your emails.

Having a clear view of your upcoming and previous manual campaigns (in your yearly send plan), and subsequently linking these to results, will let you see what has worked and what hasn't to help inform and optimise your ongoing strategy. It will also let you evaluate the content you are sending to different segments in your database and get more granular with your analysis.

Another way to optimise your current sends is to find your optimal send day or time for your regular, manually scheduled email campaigns. This will depend on your audience; for example, if you're a retailer selling to consumers that are mainly in employment, perhaps test sending mailings during the evening or at the weekends when they are more likely to be at home and perhaps have more time to browse and make a purchase. Alternatively, before or after work times, or at lunchtimes during the week when they may be on a break and perusing the internet?

Once again, stepping into your subscribers' shoes and considering who they are, what they need from you and when they need it, is the best way to optimise your results.

Increasing Your Frequency

A quick way to increase the revenue you generate from your campaigns is by adding in new emails to your strategy.

There are three main ways I suggest you do this:

1. **Increase segmentation and send more targeted emails.**

   As discussed in Chapter 1, you can use segmentation to identify sections of your database with specific attributes, interests or behaviour, to whom you can send highly relevant campaigns. This means you can send more emails to smaller sections of your audience, that are specific to their needs and are therefore more likely to see higher engagement.

2. **Add 'remail' emails to follow up important campaigns.**

   Follow up specific emails (such as those with special offers or key messages) and resend to those who didn't open or click on the first email. When you do this, make sure you change the subject line from that of the first email to try to capture their attention in a different way this time.

3. **Implement a weekly roundup email.**

   For your engaged audience (those who are interacting with your emails), consider sending a roundup email to summarise the week's top offers or content in one place, or to highlight top products, for example.

Worried about 'bombarding' your subscribers? Don't be!

Only worry if you see an increase in complaints or unsubscribes. If your content is well-timed, relevant and interesting, subscribers will welcome your communications.

Don't forget that you should also set expectations at the point of sign-up as to how many emails they should anticipate receiving from you – if they think they are receiving one a week, and start to receive one a day, for example, chances are this will be seen as too many and could result in negative engagement.

And don't forget to ask for permission when adding new email types to your send strategy.

If you're adding new recurring manual emails into your send schedule, ask subscribers to opt in to receive these additional emails (this could be done through a preference centre for example) to ensure they are actually interested in receiving them, and to stop an influx of negative engagement (which could impact your deliverability).

Crafting Copy That Converts

The content that you put into your emails, from the words you use to the imagery you display, provides the key information and prompt needed to push the reader through to take your desired action.

The next area of your content to optimise is specifically the copy itself.

Again, put the subscriber first and consider what the copy needs to do in order to meet their needs and encourage engagement.

In email, much of the supporting text is likely to be found on the landing page that the email links through to. The main task of the email content is actually to persuade an individual to click a link and find out more, rather than to make an outright purchase – as mentioned previously, your email is like a shop window leading to more information. However, with more interactive technology becoming prevalent, some functionality does exist to allow subscribers to buy right there in the inbox, and so copy is having to adapt to meet these additional needs.

When writing email copy, there are three main areas to focus in on:

1. **An attention-grabbing headline** – headlines should add to rather than simply repeat the subject line. In effect, it should provide a bridge between the subject and key message or offer.

2. **A key message** – ensure your main message is succinct, impactful and, again, captures the subscriber's attention. Particularly focus on the first line of your copy and make your main point quickly to encourage interaction. You also need to inspire a desire in your subscriber to want to read your email. When crafting your copy, always ensure you answer every reader's most important question: 'What's in it for me?'

   Carefully consider the words and phrasing in the copy and how these can influence the reader.

3. **A call-to-action** – emails are almost always sent in order to move the recipient to do something. That response varies, but the most common action required is clicking through to your website to find out more or make a purchase. Your whole email should be created to guide the subscriber to take the desired action.

The copy you use has a direct impact on the engagement with your email campaign.

When creating copy for your emails, or briefing your copywriting team, always remember to paint your content **PICTURE**:

*P*ersuasion tactics

Create a connection with your subscriber and appeal to them on an emotional level with your copy to inspire them to take your desired action.

*I*mpact

Ensure your copy has impact and really connects with your subscribers from the moment they open the email. Utilise your typography (size, colour and font of your headings, sub-headings, body copy and call-to-action text and buttons), as well as the wording you use, to create a great first impression and engage the subscriber enough to keep reading and want to find out more. Optimise the beginning of the email and increase response rates by making the proposition or offer visible in the first two lines.

*C*orrect content

Don't forget to always check your facts, prices, information and links are correct and not out of date before sending your message.

*T*ease the information

Your email should be like a shop window, offering enough information to capture their interest and encourage them into the shop (click through to your landing page) to find out more (and make a purchase). Offering too much information in the email can lead to confusion and overwhelm.

*U*nderstand your audience

Write for your target market and tailor messaging to meet their needs and solve their problems. Focus on the benefits, not just the features of your product or service and tell subscribers what is in it for them.

***R**eiterate your main message*

Throughout the copy, as well as your call-to-action, ensure that one message is the main focus and is not diluted with lots of different messages which may confuse the subscriber leading to inaction.

***E**asy to read*

Communicate your key message, briefly and simply: make it skimmable. Don't confuse subscribers by using difficult words or technical jargon. Keep content powerful and to the point.

Speaking in Your Brand Tone of Voice

This is a vital and often overlooked part of email copywriting.

Your tone of voice is the 'personality' of your brand coming through in your copy – what you say and how you say it.

In the same way as it is important to have consistent design to easily identify your brand from the look of an email, ensuring you have a clear and defined set of guidelines in place to keep your messaging consistent across your online and offline communications is also vital.

Refer to your company's style (e.g. formal or informal) as well as to your customer personas (we discuss these in the next section) to create your tone of voice guidelines, and incorporate words, phrases and a flow that will reflect your brand as well as resonate with your target audience.

Crafting a Message That's Persuasive

As with all copywriting, making a connection with the reader is vital to conveying your message effectively, and getting them to where you want them to be. Your call-to-action (CTA) buttons, sign-up form copy and email content are no different. They need to be carefully crafted and tested to ensure they wield the maximum result. Using persuasion tactics is a great way to do this.

There has been much written about different types of persuasion; perhaps the most well known are the 6 principles identified by Robert Cialdini in his book *Influence: The Psychology of Persuasion* (www.amazon.co.uk/Influence-Psychology-Robert-Cialdini-PhD/dp/006124189X), among others.

These include: **reciprocity** (exchanging something with another for mutual benefit), **consistency** (people have a need to appear consistent in their words and actions), **consensus** (people are more receptive to the opinions of others (i.e. peers) than they are to the opinion of a brand), **affinity (credibility)** (people are more likely to make decisions by comparing themselves to others who are similar to themselves), **authority** (as a well-known brand/industry leader/information provider, you are a recognised authority) and **scarcity** (the fear of loss is far greater than the desire to gain).

These types of techniques are used time and time again and have been since marketing began.

Think about the examples around you every day in the marketing you see: sales that end on a specific date, offers that are limited to only a certain number of customers or pieces available (for example, limited-edition products), and using reviews on sales pages (think about the popularity of companies such as TripAdvisor and Feefo).

When briefing your copywriters or writing copy yourself, think about how you can entice, inspire and persuade the subscriber to take your desired action using techniques such as these.

Evaluate Your Competitors

If you haven't already, I highly recommend setting up a separate email account (Microsoft, Gmail, Yahoo! etc.) and registering for your competitor's email programmes, as well as those of companies in other industries.

This is a useful tactic to learn what your competitors are doing. A client of mine did this and noticed that a competitor was starting to copy their content, design and send times – not cool! But knowing this allowed them to adjust their own strategy to keep improving and stand out.

Reviewing other email programmes is also a great source of inspiration – you never know what ideas you could gain by looking at what people outside of your industry are doing.

✎ TAKE ACTION

- Optimise your yearly send plan.

  Think about the campaigns you have planned for the next 6–12 months and follow these five steps to create, or optimise, your content schedule:

  1. Get a calendar and start by adding your regular updates (for example, regular informational newsletters, educational messages and promotional emails), as well as specialised sales emails during key company sales periods (for example, January sales) onto the calendar.

  2. Plot public holidays and key events for your organisation onto the calendar (for example, Christmas, Easter, Mother's/Father's Day etc as well as company events such as anniversaries or scheduled events you're attending).

  3. Plan backwards around these events. For example, Christmas is one of the most important times of the year for retailers. Mark key dates on your calendar around this event such as your last postage date, Black Friday and Cyber Monday etc., and plan sends around these dates.

  4. Doing the previous three steps allows you to have a high-level overview of what campaigns are sending and when – check for campaign clashes/too many emails within a time frame, and amend your schedule as necessary.

  5. Then, against each campaign you have added to the calendar, list out:

- o main content outline ideas
- o call-to-action for each
- o any images you may require

And don't forget to also make a note of:

- o WHY you are sending this email (to drive sales or engagement – for example, video views, downloads, blog reads etc.)
- o Key Performance Indicators (KPIs) to monitor success

- Brainstorm five example content buckets that you could use in your business to avoid lethargy.

- Find an example of one or two previous emails that you have sent and review the content:

  - o How could it have been better structured to encourage conversion?
  - o Could it be written in a way that is more inspiring, relevant or persuasive?
  - o Does your brand's voice clearly come through in your copy?

- Is there a way to quickly increase the frequency of your campaigns based on your current send strategy (introducing a remail for important campaigns for example)?

- Set up a separate email account (Microsoft, Gmail, Yahoo! etc.) and register for your competitor's email programmes, as well as those of companies you admire in other industries.

You can download a copy of this as a worksheet here:
www.etelligencebook.com/members/step2/sendstrategy/

2.2
Data

Now that you know what data you currently have and where it is stored within your business, we need to start further categorising this data and adding to your 'wish list'.

This involves speaking to different departments in your business that may own different sections of data. You need to find the best way to make this information available to use in your email marketing where it isn't currently, or starting to collect additional data that you know would be useful in order to further segment or personalise your content.

If it's the latter, you have to decide the best way to collect this data depending on which of the five main groups (discussed in Chapter 1.2) you want to expand on.

For example:

1. **Known data** – decide how you want to ask subscribers for more information. This could be on your initial sign-up form or through progressive profiling.

2. **Behavioural data** – specify what pages, products and actions (for example) you want to track on your website.

3. **Purchase data** – ensuring your eCommerce platform is recording and feeding through all available data for use in your ESP.

4. **Contextual data** – this will most likely require a third-party system to track this type of information, although some ESPs will be able to do this at a basic level, such as targeting by device.

5. **Cultural data** – this involves a much wider database of information and depends on what kind of connections you want to make. For example, if you want to connect different products together (by category, type, relevancy, or upsell/cross-sell options for example), you would need to have this learning mapped in your database.

When it comes to the first group, known data, there are two main ways to do this:

1. Collecting data as part of the initial sign-up process

The first step in the subscriber journey is to opt in to receive your emails.

At this point, the most important action is to gain permission to send marketing communications and at least the basic data you need to continue that conversation – primarily their email address.

The general rule when it comes to sign-up forms is that the more data you ask for, the less people will complete the action; however, those that do give this additional information will be more highly qualified (you will know more about them and are better able to target them with relevant information – you know how close to being your ideal customer they are, for example).

So, with this in mind, you need to consider what you want to collect from the start of the relationship that is going to assist you in creating a personalised, targeted communications strategy to maximise your relationship with the subscriber.

In most cases, businesses choose to just collect an email address; I would always advise collecting at least the subscriber's name in addition to this. Including their name in communications helps to build trust from the very first message.

But it's also worth considering the following question: *'What is the business-critical data you need to collect from the start of the relationship?'*

For example, if you are a retail company selling clothing, I would consider it business-critical information to ask the subscriber what they are interested in – men's, women's or children's clothing.

This information allows you to immediately better target the offers and information you send to them, increasing your relevancy and, in turn, your results.

There are two main ways to approach collecting data here:

i. A one-step sign-up process

    The standard way to present your opt-in – one form that, when submitted, takes you to a Thank You page and the process is complete.

ii. A two-step or chained sign-up process

    This involves submitting the first stage of the form, and then offering the subscriber a secondary form (or series of additional short forms) where they can provide more information.

    My advice when using this type of form would be to ensure that the opt-in is registered after the submission of the first step of the form, and the following stages are voluntary.

With both of these options, it is also worth considering which data is mandatory (for example, email address and name) in order to submit the form, vs. information that is voluntary – this can also help with your form conversion rates.

Remember: only collect the information you NEED – if you're not going to use it, don't collect it.

2. Progressive profiling

This tactic involves collecting more data about the subscriber as you move through your relationship with them (beyond the sign-up). There are various ways you can do this including:

- **Sending out a subscriber survey**

  In order to get the most people possible to complete your survey use the following tips:

  o Let people know how long the survey will take – be honest and keep it short! Try and keep it to under 5 minutes to make it as accessible as possible and easy to complete.

  o Tell the subscriber WHY you want them to complete the survey – for example, to help make the email communications you send more relevant to them.

  o Don't send out a survey too often – if you're always asking for help, people will be unlikely to complete every request. However, I would recommend checking in with your subscribers once or twice a year to ensure your programme is still interesting, relevant and helpful to them.

  o Make sure you analyse and use the information you receive back from your survey!

- **Using in-email polls**

  This is a very shortened version of a survey consisting of just one question asked right within the email content. The answer options given will be individually tracked links, so that depending on which one is clicked, this can be recorded accordingly as the subscriber's answer.

  This option offers a really quick way to get feedback on an individual aspect of your programme such as a specific email type or offer.

- **Offering a preference centre**

  A preference centre offers subscribers the chance to update their personal information and make choices about the communications they receive from you. It allows you to:

  o increase data known about subscribers in order to provide a more personalised, relevant experience.

  o offer choice in communication preferences – let them have more control over what they receive from you and when, to suit their needs and interests.

  o provide an alternative to a complete unsubscribe for those who may be choosing to stop receiving emails for reasons that are within your control to change – such as email frequency or type of content they are receiving from you.

  o offer different communications options to expand your marketing reach – for example, gain opt-ins for email/post/SMS communications.

  o remind subscribers of the benefits of receiving emails from you.

When creating a preference centre, consider:

o providing the opportunity to choose how many of each message type they wish to receive over a weekly or monthly basis. Ensure that each message type is described clearly.

o allowing them to take control of the timing of the emails they receive:

    — Offer a digest email option for those subscribers who do not want to receive emails more than once a week/month for example.

    — Allow subscribers to take a break from communications for two weeks/one month/two months for example.

o letting them tell you more about themselves and their interests to gain more information and extend the opportunity for you to increase your segmentation and personalisation in the future.

Don't forget to ask only for information you will use to personalise your communications and offers going forward! Ensure you make the options simple to understand and the benefits of giving the additional information easy to ascertain.

Knowing Who You Want to Target – Creating Your Customer Personas

In order to create a targeted, engaged email list full of people who are more likely to buy from you, you need to attract the right kind of people onto your list.

The first and most important step in doing this is to create a customer persona (also called an avatar) – a detailed view of exactly who you are targeting and who your ideal person is to attract to your business and buy from you.

Speak to one person or you're speaking to no one.

Creating your customer persona is about bringing together an image of who that person is, what they need, what is going on in their lives, the actions they take regularly and the help that they need.

You are effectively segmenting different groups of prospects (different customer types) by attributes that they share in common.

If you don't know who your target audience is and what makes them tick, the conversions to opt in that you see from your sign-up forms, and to purchase from your email campaigns, won't be maximised, because the content you provide and how you communicate with them won't resonate properly.

In order to gain maximum conversions for minimum budget, you need to speak to just one type of person at a time with your messaging.

In any business you may have multiple customer types that you are targeting. It's important to understand and distinguish between these when it comes to providing the right information to move them through their journey – to allow you to connect with them in the right way, using the right wording and imagery, for example.

But focus in on one at a time – make your sign-up forms, offers and advertising strategy targeted to one of them.

You can create other forms and other campaigns for other personas going forward.

For example, imagine you are a pizza company. Many people like pizza and therefore you may think 'I'm a business that targets everybody!' But you're not!

With each piece of marketing you need to have a specific person – your ideal customer persona – in mind (and in this business, you will have multiple), such as:

- couples
- families with children
- groups of friends eating together

Each of these customer personas will have differing needs, wants and habits that you will need to target with different targeting of ads, imagery and wording to resonate with them.

For example, you may create separate TV ads targeting each persona, each running on different channels and at different times:

- targeting TV programmes such as *The Big Bang Theory* or *Game of Thrones* featuring a group of friends or couples talking about/ ordering/eating pizza

- targeting TV programmes such as Saturday night entertainment or mid-week primetime soaps featuring a family eating pizza with messaging such as 'save on the washing up' or 'enjoy more time together without having to cook'.

Think about TV ads that you've seen recently – you've probably seen both of these examples!

If you know exactly who you want to attract, you can create appealing content that truly engages and excites or helps them in some way.

This is why it is so important to really get to know your audience – to understand them, their commonalities and their needs.

This should be done at a wider business level, but I'd also like you to use this information and drill down even further from an email marketing perspective.

Think about areas such as:

- **Who is this customer persona?**

  Demographic information such as age/gender/salary range/job title etc. It is advisable to give your avatar a name and put a picture to them to help you bring them to life. That way, when you are targeting them you can think, 'I'm speaking to Jane – she's 35 years old and works for a multinational eCommerce company as the marketing director. She has worked for the company for three to five years and has a team of ten.' You want to build a really clear picture in your head of who this 'person' is so that you can find the words, imagery and offers that really resonate with them.

- **Where they can be found?**

  Online/offline (for example, specific websites/blogs they visit, social media channels they regularly use, TV programmes they watch, magazines/newspapers they read etc.).

- **What 'keeps them up at night'?**

  What worries them? What drives them? What would they like to achieve in their life/business? What problems are they facing that your product/service could help solve?

- **What is their buying behaviour?**

  Do they regularly shop online? Search Google first? Look on price comparison websites?

  Gather information relevant to your company about that persona – such as the types of products they are most likely to buy from you, their behaviour in regards to your products/services, their purchase behaviour, as well as how often they buy, dependency on using discounts or vouchers, their attitude towards buying your product/ service online, the top reason/time they would purchase your product/service etc.

There are lots of resources online to help you do this, but what you will need is to gather data on your audience – for use in creating your customer personas in the first place, as well as to identify them in your database and be able to target them in your email campaigns.

Your customer personas can link directly to your use of segmentation IF you are able to identify these prospects within your database. This type of information can be used by every department in your business to better understand your customers.

Many companies don't have the data available to do this successfully – if you find yourself in this situation, think about the data you need to collect to start better identifying personas in your database.

✎ TAKE ACTION

- Expand your thinking from Chapter 1 and further explore the data that you would like to have available to use in your email campaign strategy.

- Then consider how you can collect this data from your subscribers (on sign-up/in-email poll/survey or preference centre).

Data Type	Data Field	How Will It Be Collected?
Known data	Interested in: • men's clothing • women's clothing • children's clothing	On sign-up (one-step registration form)

- Find out if you already have customer personas created within your business.

- If you don't have them created already, create an initial customer persona:

  o Start with one customer type to begin with (you can then create further customer types after you have completed this one).

  o Think about areas such as:
     – Who is this avatar?
     – Where can they be found?
     – What 'keeps them up at night'?
     – What is their buying behaviour?

o   What data would you need to collect in your business in order to target your personas within your database?

You can download a copy of this as a worksheet here: www.etelligencebook.com/members/step2/data/

2.3
Segmentation and Personalisation

Once you have conducted your audit and know what segmentation you are currently using, as well as the data you have available (or would like to collect in the future to allow for more granular segmentation), you can start to create a more defined segmentation strategy to really make yourself stand out in the inbox and have an even bigger impact with your messages.

The best way to start optimising your segmentation strategy is to focus on the areas of your database that have the most commonalities and those that will provide the most revenue opportunities.

For example, an eCommerce company with no previous segmentation may want to start by segmenting those who have previously purchased from them against those who haven't. Or creating a segment of subscribers who have purchased once from the company and not again.

You can then use this data to communicate with subscribers differently; the information needing to be conveyed to those who have not purchased before (why they should buy from you, credibility, how to purchase etc.) will be different from those who are already familiar with you.

If you already have some segmentation as part of your strategy, there is always room to improve what you are doing and expand your reach – *now is the time to really start using the data you have in a clever way to better target and engage your audience.* For example, could you look deeper into the value of your customers by conducting RFM (Recency, Frequency, Monetary) analysis and targeting them differently depending on these factors?

The ability to segment email lists and individualise email campaign messaging are the most effective personalisation tactics for 51% and 50% of marketing influencers respectively.
(Source: Ascend2, 2016)[6]

There is an overwhelming number of ways you can segment your list. But it is not only the segmentation criteria you use that are going make the impact; the content you include in those emails that are sent to these segments is critical to ensuring an engaging campaign, as is the time at which you send it.

It comes back to the three elements of a successful email campaign we've touched on already:

Sending the right message, to the right person, at the right time.

The key to a good segmentation strategy is effective planning and execution of all the elements involved. Again, you really need to know your audience, what makes them 'tick' and what is going to resonate with them – the segmentation just gives you even more of a direction to steer your copy and offers to support this.

Well thought-out segments and relevant content = higher results.

Basic vs. More Advanced Segmentation Techniques

Basic segmentation relies on the data fields you store in your list, either used individually (for example, segmenting male vs. female subscribers, or purchasers vs. non-purchasers) or taking it one step further and beginning to layer these together (for example, selecting subscribers who have purchased a specific item and opened one of your emails within the last three months – combining purchase data and email activity).

To take your segmentation strategy one step further, start to add additional layers and further combine your segmentation criteria to get more granular and therefore, more targeted and relevant with the messaging you are sending to these subscribers. The possibilities of who you can target in this way are almost endless. The only limiting factor will be the data you have access to, the resources available and, of course, your imagination!

However, becoming truly advanced in this technique involves understanding what the subscriber needs and wants, and to offer this information before they even know they need it themselves in some cases.

When you are ready to use smarter, more advanced segmentation, consider using analysis based on techniques such as:

- **the subscriber's position in the customer journey** (we'll break this down in more detail in Chapter 3) – this will allow you to not only speak to their current needs but anticipate their next steps in the journey and provide information to help them navigate this process more successfully.

- **identifying and targeting your customer personas** – by collecting additional data, customer personas will be easier to identify within the email marketing database, allowing for further segmentation based on this crucial information and therefore, a greater connection with subscribers.

- **propensity modelling** – this involves calculating the likelihood of someone taking an action (for example, buying a specific product) based on what others have done. If you can offer up suggestions to help the subscriber extend the relationship with you (in purchasing more, more frequently for example) you can increase the revenue you generate from them by anticipating their needs.

- **using RFM (Recency, Frequency, Monetary) analysis** – rather than just based on previous purchases, look at value of those purchases (individual and overall), frequency of purchases, customer loyalty etc. to identify the most and least valuable clients within your database and target them with offers accordingly.

Each of these techniques once again puts the subscriber at the very heart of your email marketing strategy which subsequently generates increased engagement and revenue for your business.

Don't forget: when segmenting your list, ensure a sufficient audience size can still be reached to maximise impact whilst providing increased relevancy. If your segment is too small, the cost and time of creating multiple campaigns may outweigh the possible return.

The most important factor when optimising your segmentation strategy is to review which data fields and combination of data fields create the segments that have the biggest impact on your results and revenue. Always test and improve your segmentation plan as you try new combinations.

✎ TAKE ACTION

- Devise a more defined segmentation strategy:

  o Think about the data you currently have and the data you plan on collecting in the future – which fields could be used to segment your database and start providing more targeted communications?

  o How will you use this data? Will you use it to create groups to send specific campaigns to? Will you use it to personalise your email content through the use of dynamic fields or dynamic content?

  o How can you combine this data to create more granular segments to target?

    – Are you able to identify customer personas from the data you have?

    – Do you have the resources available to conduct RFM analysis or implement propensity modelling?

  o Consider the type of content you could send that would be most appropriate for these new segments.

- Assess which of these segments are going to be most worthwhile for your business to implement. Create a grid of options, ranking their cost to implement vs. their possible impact on your results.

  This will allow you to identify the 'quick wins' that you can implement quickly and easily and will have a significant impact, as opposed to those that need more resources and time to implement.

See Appendix 4 on page 302 for an example.

- Create a segmentation strategy roadmap – the actions you will take and when, to optimise your current strategy

  For example:

Stage 1	**Get correct data in place** Prioritise: • purchase data • behavioural data • known data **Analyse data to gain additional insight** • anticipated data/Artificial Intelligence (AI) **Implement preference centre/collecting data on sign-up forms**
Stage 2	**Identify segments** • customer journey stage • customer type • customer personas • email activity
Stage 3	**Plan new campaigns/segments** Prioritise: • content within weekly emails to increase relevancy • triggered campaigns such as welcome programme/reactivation/automatic reminders/browse abandon etc. • personalised content in campaigns
Stage 4	**Implement new campaigns/segments**

You can download a copy of this as a worksheet here:
www.etelligencebook.com/members/step2/segmentation/

eFOCUS Marketing

CLIENT CASE STUDY

Client Type: Travel provider

Objective: Increase awareness of new set of brochures and drive orders.

Situation

As a nationwide travel provider, our client relies on the launch of their new brochures every six months to drive a large uplift in their sales and to support the process throughout the rest of the year.

At each launch, different types of brochure are created to cater for various travel destinations, highlighting different trips available, for both consumers and trade clients.

With only generic email campaigns sent on previous launches, our client was keen to see the impact of a new segmentation strategy on their engagement and conversion rates (to order a copy of the new brochure).

Challenges

This client had been sending generic email campaigns for previous brochure launches and had started to see new orders decreasing. Their bookings rested on being able to get the brochures and offers in front of the right people.

The main challenge was in creating differing designs and send strategies to cater for each newly created segment that would resonate to increase engagement and orders.

This project was all about using the data held about the subscriber, their previous behaviour and known preferences, as well as their customer type, to present relevant information accordingly.

Also key was ensuring the design of the email was optimised to capture attention using placement of imagery and the information provided.

Solution

In the weeks leading up to the launch of the new brochures, a series of three emails was broadcast to key data segments: past passengers, prospects, and trade.

The wording shown on each of these emails was changed using dynamic content to specifically engage with each segment using targeted language, key points and imagery.

Specific landing pages were also created to give more information when clicking through from emails, as well as direct links to order each brochure.

Each email broadcast was also subject to A/B split testing around subject lines used, call-to-action button wording and the amount of copy included, in order to ensure each send was optimised.

The results of this work spoke for themselves – open rates reached between 21 and 34% (an increase of over 50% in some cases), click rates between 6 and 11% and, most impressively, there was a 350% year-on-year increase in brochure orders.

Getting Personal with Your Subscribers to Increase Your Results

Personalisation should go beyond just referencing the recipient's first name.

As we've already discussed, true personalisation is about knowing what your customers' wants and needs are, sometimes before they even know themselves! Segmenting your list to send relevant communications is a big step towards doing this – the next is to further adapt your content, not just to target these groups, but to provide information, education and recommendations on a 1-2-1 basis, based on that recipient's profile, interests or behaviour.

What you are able to achieve really does come down to the data you hold in your systems, not only directly about the subscriber, but also about the surrounding cultural data you hold to be able to connect this data to the real world around them.

80% of consumers like it when emails they receive from retailers recommend products to them based on previous purchases.
(Source: Internet Retailer)[7]

But product recommendations aren't just a preference; they lead to an increase in sales.

The inclusion of personalised recommendations in email campaigns and product pages increased sales by 3.5%.
(Source: Fresh Relevance)[8]

Your Data Hierarchy

There are different levels of data that allow you to personalise your email marketing campaigns to varying degrees, including the five data groups we've already discussed plus one more:

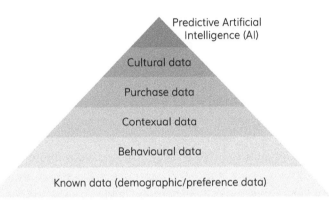

Predictive Artificial Intelligence (AI)

Cultural data

Purchase data

Contexual data

Behavioural data

Known data (demographic/preference data)

At the bottom of the hierarchy is your *known data* – we see this here because it can change, but you'll only know about it if a subscriber updates their information. So it's not the most reliable.

Consider this – a subscriber tells you that they are moving house in the next six months. When they first give you this data, it is extremely valuable up-to-date information that you can use to target your product recommendations, offers and information around this life event. However, as soon as the subscriber moves house, this information is instantly out of date.

As you move up the hierarchy, the data becomes more relevant – the products/categories/blogs/videos that people view on your website (on-site behaviour) tell you a lot about what they are looking to buy right now, whereas their purchase behaviour gives you the opportunity to upsell items around what they have already bought.

For example, providing product recommendations based on the last products/categories a customer browsed on your website can be an extremely powerful tool in linking the content of your email into the subscriber's real life and what they NEED RIGHT NOW, and what they are actively looking to purchase.

Contextual data is highly relevant because it feeds into what's happening in their lives at the time of opening the email, and *cultural data* talks directly to elements that connect your recommendations together and make them more real to the subscriber's situation (for example, product recommendations based on where they live and regional preferences).

At the top of the hierarchy, we see predictive suggestions in the form of *AI and Machine Learning* – the data set we haven't discussed yet.

Building an email programme that uses AI or Machine Learning to predict and serve the right content to your subscriber, based on what they are most likely to interact with, is the nirvana of personalisation – and something that the majority of companies are not currently doing or able to do.

But by predicting what a subscriber will be most likely to engage with, you can offer your subscribers the products, services and information they need before they even know they need it.

To implement this technique, you need to take information from every other section of the hierarchy to analyse and, based on what other people have done previously or associated cultural or contextual data in particular, make an educated assumption as to what that subscriber is likely to do next. This allows you to serve the most appropriate content and offers to encourage the subscriber to buy.

Conducting this type of analysis and implementing it into your strategy in its fullest form is complex and time-consuming, not to mention costly in a lot of cases. Which is why most businesses have not been able to implement it into their programmes yet. However, even at a basic, first-stage level, most businesses are able to pull in some level of prediction into their strategy, for example, offering "customers who purchased [this product] also purchased these items" or other recommended products based on browse behaviour – complementary or alternative suggestions.

There are many systems out there that have the ability to use the data you know about your subscribers to serve them content relevant to their current situation (and much more!) to varying degrees.

Why It's Important to Sometimes Take a Considered Approach to Your Email Personalisation and Targeting

There are many examples where personalisation has caused more harm than good; most notably the example where Target, a large US department store, found 'clues' to a teenage customer's possible pregnancy, based on data gathered (purchase and demographic information held about the subscriber), even before she had told her father.

When creating your personalisation and targeting strategy consider how your content will come across to your subscribers – could it cause offence or upset? For example, if you are creating an algorithm as in the case of the Target example, to focus in on consumers at different stages of their pregnancy without getting this information directly from them, is this likely to be 100% correct in all situations? What if that person suffers the loss of the baby, is a surrogate or hasn't told their family yet of their impending news?! If you were buying an engagement ring online, would you then want to be remarketed to with 'you browsed this, so we thought you might like this...' suggestions?

There are always circumstances in which your personalisation will need to be carefully considered and perhaps more subtly delivered to the customer (in amongst other products for example).

It's also important to consider how your personalisation could go wrong in terms of the data you hold. For example, if you are sending out a summary email that relays back to the subscriber how many times they have bought from you over the last year and that number comes out as zero, this would be a good time to exclude them from receiving that campaign and target them with a different piece of content (and probably an offer to purchase from you).

Think about how can you ensure the way in which you target subscribers and speak to them is not 'creepy' or 'stalkerish'. No one likes to think they are being tracked and followed!

Instead, consider how you can make your personalisation helpful and relevant.

✎ TAKE ACTION

- Consider your current personalisation strategy and how you can further optimise it to increase the relevancy of your campaigns. Think about:

    o What data are you able to use for personalisation that you are not already using?

    o What technology do you have in place (or could put in place to help you analyse your data and provide more relevant information/product recommendations for example)?

    Discover a list of technology providers you may want to explore here:
    www.etelligencebook.com/members/step2/personalisation/

    o Are you targeting your messaging, images and offers correctly for your ideal customer persona?

    o Are you thinking about how your personalisation could be perceived by the subscriber – check it's not being implemented in a 'creepy' way, but is instead helpful.

    o Which campaigns you're already sending could benefit from increased personalisation (either using dynamic fields or dynamic content in some way)?

CASE STUDY

Client Type: Fitness equipment retailer

Objective: To reduce spend by consolidating three solutions into one and drive more value from personalisation.

Situation

Fitness Superstore is the largest specialist fitness equipment retailer in the UK. Its fast-growing eCommerce business is supported by 10 stores across the UK – its flagship store in Northampton is the largest fitness showroom in Europe.

Most sales come from home users, but they also sell directly to gyms. Its audience ranges from fitness fanatics to people looking to improve their health.

Challenges

Fitness Superstore were using three different solutions to deliver personalisation. They had one solution for email marketing, one for website product recommendations, and a third for pop-ups and abandonment emails.

The marketing team needed to consolidate these into one solution that covered all their existing personalisation requirements, with the added benefit of a single point of contact for support.

The Solution

Working with Pure360 has allowed them to bring all their needs under one roof, simplifying the management and helping the team focus on driving more value from personalisation.

Fitness Superstore have taken full advantage of Pure360's eCommerce solution, which combines email and website personalisation with behavioural targeting.

Within the solution, the team is able to deliver highly personalised website experiences based on browsing activity, purchase history, and interaction with email campaigns.

Pure360's machine learning powered recommendation engine ensures that each customer is shown relevant products while they browse and within email campaigns. On top of this, Fitness Superstore wanted to ensure its product recommendations were driving the highest possible business value. Pure360 helped them undertake custom work that increased average order values by upselling premium products with higher margins.

Pure360's testing capabilities were vital for the team. They use A/B testing to find the highest converting email subject lines and products placed within the emails. They also use A/B testing on product pages to see which types of product recommendations have the highest conversion rate.

Before choosing Pure360, the marketing team were reliant on their previous vendors to make even the smallest changes to their personalisation programmes. For example, changing the content in a cart abandonment email.

Now they have the complete freedom to make any changes they want, whenever they want. This allows them to react quickly to noticeable trends and strive for continual optimisation.

Pure360's singular solution allowed Fitness Superstore to bring together multiple datasets to deliver intelligent personalisation. This included website browsing behaviour, personal preferences, purchase history, and email engagement.

2.4

Automated Campaign Strategy

Automating campaigns within your business allows you to set up tasks, not only to send email campaigns, but also within your wider marketing and sales function, to make generating new leads and sales more effective and efficient.

This process is called *marketing automation* and brings the opportunity to continuously develop a consistent relationship with the subscriber on auto-pilot.

Using marketing automation within your business also allows you to:

- build marketing lists and nurture prospects automatically with personalised email messages.

- follow up on on-site activities like browsing products and content with highly relevant communications.

- review interaction with messages or online content, and segment your list around the user's level of intent to purchase, based on lead scoring techniques, for example (we'll discuss this further in Chapter 3).

- learn about your prospects and customers with increased data and predictive analytics in order to advance your messaging strategy.

- integrate your channels to look at a prospect's behaviour in order to increase the relevancy of your communications, bringing together your social tools, website, SMS and overall CRM data.

- pass alerts to your sales team when the time is right.

- create more relevant experiences and offers to give an increase in Return-on-Investment (ROI) from communications.

- increase efficiency in marketing teams, saving time on campaigns which were previously deployed manually.

Marketing automation offers businesses the potential to automate the delivery of new, more sophisticated processes and relevant communications, over a range of touchpoints and channels across the customer journey.

The Customer Journey

When you are identifying triggers for campaigns (for example, what data will start an email or series of emails sending to subscribers such as time since last purchase, a birthday, or an action such as abandoning products in an online basket), it is important to consider when they are being sent in relation to the customer journey (also known as a lifecycle).

In this instance we are primarily talking about using email marketing to target these stages. But of course, true marketing automation is all about integrating all of your data, creating a single customer view to allow you to see behaviour across other channels and target your messages accordingly.

You should also ensure that the messaging in your marketing channels is consistent with your business across all touchpoints, whether that be through your social media channels, website, SMS, display advertising, print advertising or other channels.

A classic customer journey model is made up of five key stages as shown below. Each stage represents a step or thought process that the potential customer goes through with your business, throughout the life of their interactions with you.

It is important to plan campaigns at each stage to target subscribers effectively with relevant communications tailored to the information that will be most relevant to them at that time, to help encourage them on to the next stage.

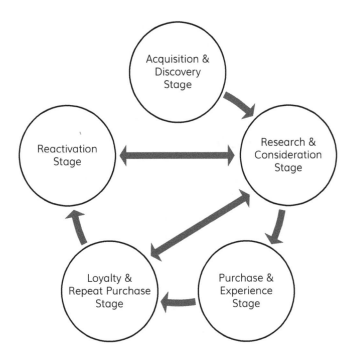

Let's look at each stage individually from an email marketing perspective.

Acquisition Stage

Aim: to attract, welcome and start building the relationship with new subscribers.

Key behaviour: a subscriber finds your sign-up form, subscribes and starts their relationship with you.

They are looking to find out more about why they should shop with you, your credibility, if they can trust in the service you provide and if you have the kinds of product/service they may be looking for.

They may not be specifically looking for anything yet (they may not know exactly what they want) or they may have found you because they were searching for something specific (or at least a category of product/ service types) and are moving towards the next stage and deciding whether or not to make a purchase.

Example: in this stage, think about how to optimise your sign-up process to capture their attention and maximise conversion to opt-in, as well as implementing a welcome and on-boarding email programme – a targeted series of emails to introduce the new subscriber to your brand and offerings and set expectations over the first 30 days of the relationship.

Research and Consideration Stage

Aim: to help the new subscriber make the decision as to which product to buy, and why they would benefit from purchasing from your company.

Key behaviour: having found you, the subscriber now needs to be educated, inspired and helped to make the right purchase decision for them.

Consider the categories of products/services or the specific items they are browsing on your website, the blog posts they are viewing and the other pages they are navigating to.

For example, if someone is viewing your FAQs or delivery information, they are telling you they are looking for more information to help them make their decision, related to how your company operates. Browsing multiple products in the same category (for example, lots of different skirts within women's clothing) tells you that's the product type they require, but they haven't yet found the perfect one for them. Viewing different types of blog posts tells you they are looking for inspiration, and looking at multiple posts in the same topic area tells you exactly what they are researching.

In this stage, you will also see more specific behaviour, such as searching for certain products, registering for back-in-stock notifications or adding items to their basket but not going on to purchase.

Example: campaigns sent at this stage may include communications to a subscriber that hasn't purchased within a specific number of days after signing up, but has shown certain behaviour on site.

This part of the journey will also include following up on-site behaviour such as browsing a specific product or category, with a targeted series of emails to help them make the decision to purchase, or you could support an abandoned basket action with a reminder to purchase or other related product recommendations. You will also send regular promotional emails and newsletters to educate and inspire subscribers.

Purchase and Experience Stage

Aim: to make the purchase process as easy as possible and give customers the best experience after buying from you.

Key behaviour: a customer decides on the product/service that's right for them and goes through your purchase portal, confirming their transaction.

They then await the delivery of their product/service (either physically or online in the case of systems access or information, for example).

When their purchase arrives, how they feel about it, start to use it and follow up with your company (for example, providing reviews) are all part of this stage.

Example: campaigns here will include transactional emails (such as purchase and despatch confirmation emails) and a post-purchase follow-up series (for example, review requests), as well as helpful content to make the most of their purchase. This is a key step in building the relationship with the customer and ensuring an excellent experience that most companies neglect; instead they only service the basic communications needed in this stage.

Offering upsell/cross-sell items here can also be helpful to enhance the experience.

The most important communications (alongside those messages that have to be sent to confirm stages of the purchase process) again involve putting the customer first – think about how you can go above and beyond to give them a fantastic experience of buying from you.

Can you provide additional information following the purchase, to help them make the most of their items?

This could include showing them how to use the item properly (perhaps a short video or blog post), looking at the most common reasons customers return items and trying to combat these in your messaging, or providing FAQs for common queries.

Loyalty and Repeat Purchase Stage

Aim: to keep the subscriber engaged and encourage them to make a repeat purchase.

Key behaviour: this stage sees first-time customers going on to make a second purchase, and a third, and a fourth and so on.

They may become advocates for your brand and share their purchase experience with friends and family, or on social media for example.

This stage is very similar to the Research and Consideration stage and many campaigns that you plan will not differ much between the two: aiming to educate, excite and inspire them towards their next purchase.

The thought process is the same for the customer before each purchase: what do I want to buy and is this the right company to buy it from?

The difference from the initial purchase is that they now know they can trust you as a company as they have bought from you before. This is also why the previous stage (Purchase and Experience) is so important to get right and take beyond just the basic transactional communications that have to be sent, in order to help bolster this next, repeat purchase phase.

Example: specific emails based on data you have about your subscriber including a birthday email or an anniversary of purchase email – campaigns that build loyalty and make the customer feel special.

You will also want to include campaigns that encourage a repeat purchase such as replenishment reminders for those products that run out (beauty products or razors for example), and further cross- and upsell campaigns based on the last purchase.

Your standard promotional mailings will also fall into this category in the crossover between this and the Research and Consideration stage. However, think about how you can adjust these to make them more customised to the increased data you now have about these customers and their previous behaviour, perhaps using dynamic content to address them as previous customers or make product suggestions based on items they've already purchased, for example.

Reactivation Stage

Aim: to identify and re-engage subscribers and purchasers who have become, or are becoming, inactive with your brand.

Key behaviour: there are two sides to this stage:

1. *Inactive subscribers:* subscribers who have become inactive with the email programme (haven't opened or clicked on your campaigns within a certain amount of time, for example nine months).

2. *Inactive customers:* customers who are no longer buying from you (haven't made another purchase within a specified amount of time – this will differ depending on your business and the average purchase frequency you would expect).

Example: implement an inactive subscriber reactivation series – a series of emails designed to re-engage a user who has not engaged with your email programme within a certain amount of time. You should also set up a series of emails to encourage inactive customers to come back and make another purchase.

In Chapter 3, we'll look at each of these in a little more detail and how to identify each stage through your data.

But for now, you should aim to start with at least one campaign in each area of the customer journey to target your subscribers — look at the campaigns you already have in place that you wrote down during your task in Chapter 1 and consider how you can optimise these. This could be adjusting the timing at which they are triggered, the content within them or the personalisation used, for example.

Planning Automated Campaigns

When planning your automated campaigns for each stage, consider these six key questions:

1. What will be the trigger that starts the email/series sending?

2. What are the criteria that subscribers must meet in order to be eligible for that trigger (i.e. which segment of your audience)?

3. How long after that trigger has been activated will the emails start sending?

4. How many emails will be in the series? Just one or multiple emails over time? If so, what is the time delay between each email?

5. What will the content of the email(s) be?

6. What is your conversion prompt? What is the overall goal of the series and what do you want them to do in each email to achieve this?

Once you have a plan in place, plot your automated campaigns onto the customer journey to quickly see if areas are sufficiently covered, as well as additional areas that could be targeted with new campaigns to encourage subscribers to the next stage. (You can see an example of this here: www.etelligencebook.com/members/step2/automatedcampaigns/)

Changing the timing of an automated campaign trigger or adding additional emails to your series can be the key to making the results you already see even better.

For example, an abandoned basket campaign: does the first email get the most engagement when triggered one hour, two hours, three hours or four hours after the action? Do you send one email, two, three, four or more emails in a series for maximum impact?

Test these differences to see what works for your subscribers.

✎ TAKE ACTION

- At each of stage of the customer journey, consider the campaigns you already have in place that you listed in your audit from Chapter 1 and think about how you can optimise these to best serve your subscribers.

- To add to your marketing strategy document, map out each of your current automated campaigns in detail:

Email # in series	Timing	Topic	Conversion	Notes
1				
2				
3				
4				

Using a post-sign-up welcome and on-boarding series for an eCommerce retailer, **see Appendix 5 on page 304 for an example** of how this may look (add as much information as possible). This will allow you to analyse each email and consider how it can be improved.

- Once you have mapped out each series, get a copy of each email and consider how the design, layout, content and trigger timing of each could be improved.

  Think about the important information that subscribers need to know at each stage to help them move forward in their journey and how you can optimise your current communications (we'll be looking at adding in new campaigns in Chapter 3 – for now, consider how you can make any campaigns you are currently sending at each stage better).

For example, can you add additional information that would help the subscriber during the Research and Consideration stage, or further inspire them?

Can you add content into your abandoned basket email that addresses key concerns they may have about purchasing from you? If you only have one email triggering here already, could you extend this series to three emails?

Could you adjust the timing of the automations currently being sent for a better impact?

Don't forget, not all of the campaigns in each stage will be automated (for example your regular promotional emails that will appear within the Research and Consideration/Loyalty and Repeat Purchase stages). But for the purposes of this task, focus on your automated campaigns.

* If you want to take this one step further, bring in ideas for campaigns sent through other marketing channels that can support your email marketing – for example, sending SMS as part of a product re-order series, or adding a printed leaflet into customer packages with an offer to encourage their next purchase. *

You can download a copy of this as a worksheet here:
www.etelligencebook.com/members/step2/automatedcampaigns/

CASE STUDY

Client Type: Funeral directors

Objective: To deliver a more efficient communication service for its clients through branding and workflow automation, freeing up executive resource and generating more revenue.

Situation
FDLIC offers support to funeral home clients nationwide by providing individually branded e-newsletters targeted to their funeral home customers. This valuable loyalty service enables their clients to establish and maintain communication with customers, while building brand awareness for both the funeral home and FDLIC.

At the time of engagement, this programme was being administered through another ESP without automation or dynamic content functionality. This required the work of a full-time FDLIC staffer, who was following an inefficient process.

Challenges
ResponseGenius provided a sophisticated, dynamic workflow email campaign solution that allowed FDLIC to completely automate their 12-month bereavement series. They coupled the

subscription workflow with individually branded dynamic content for hundreds of separate funeral home brands and agents. These two combined solutions allowed FDLIC to automate their e-newsletter delivery without constant re-creation of monthly files, campaigns and branding customisations.

The Solution

ResponseGenius streamlined and optimised the entire delivery of digital support programmes for FDLIC, allowing FDLIC staff to redirect their attention to marketing strategy development. FDLIC was able to jump the curve to become a market leader in digital communication support of clients.

Since this programme began, FDLIC has developed and launched additional digital messaging support programmes through the same approach, providing greater ancillary client programmes and meaningful incremental revenue/profit to the company.

Today, rather than having one person devote full-time hours only to managing their 12-month bereavement series, FDLIC has expanded its e-service offerings to include additional ancillary products, which now round out a complete digital marketing strategy the company can offer to its clients.

2.5
Design

You have just seconds to capture the attention of your subscriber and interest them enough to take action.

The best way to do that is to ensure that the content you send is highly relevant by using the information you know about them – either targeted to one specific segment, or by using dynamic content to automatically change content customised to the recipient.

The copy you use has a direct impact on engagement, as well as the placement and presentation of this information within your design. Your aim is to capture the subscriber's attention and direct them towards the key message and the action you want them to take.

This starts from the moment the subscriber first sees your email.

Capturing Attention in the Inbox

There are three main elements visible in the inbox that have an impact on whether or not your email even gets opened. These are:

1. **'From' name** – this identifies who the email is being sent from (not your email address but the name that is shown in the inbox). Ensure it is easily and instantly recognisable and consistent across your communications to engender trust.

   Some people recommend using a person's name here, which can work in some cases particularly for B2B companies or where the messages are more customer service based – for example, 'Kate at eFocus Marketing'.

However, in the majority of cases for B2C companies, in my experience, using a person's name can be confusing at best and misleading at worst. Your brand name is your public persona and this should be used as your 'from' name so that your messages can be instantly recognised and trusted as being from your company.

2. **Subject line** – this is one of the main elements that has an impact on whether or not an email is opened.

Many successful brands actually craft their subject line before they put together the final content for their email – it's that important! If your email doesn't get opened, people won't see the content within and have a chance to act.

Email subject lines are similar to newspaper or blog headlines in that they need to be snappy, punchy, and evoke the interest of the reader. When writing subject lines, always consider previous examples that have worked well, to build on success and ensure you do not repeat them too frequently.

You should also consider the length of your subject lines. Long subject lines can sometimes be useful in providing a little more information and getting highly interested people opening and engaging with your email. However, many mobile devices wrap the subject line at around 35 characters (as opposed to around 60 characters on desktop), so you should ensure that you front-load the most important information to make it visible in the majority of cases.

Most importantly, do not mislead the subscriber with your subject line; ensure it reflects the content of the email.

Common techniques for subject line formats include:

o **the teaser** – e.g. 'Is she fruity or nutty?'

o **the question** – e.g. 'Want to know the guaranteed price of your car?'

o **loss aversion** – e.g. 'HURRY – last chance to save ££s before the show opens.'

o **the event tie-in** – e.g. 'Spoil your dad this Father's Day!'

o **the direct approach** – e.g. 'Get 2 pairs of shoes for £49.'

o **using numbers** – e.g. '3 ways to wear this season's key trends.'

o **personalisation** – e.g. Adding a subscriber's first name, referencing a product/service they have just bought, or highlighting the area they live in, depending on the data you hold.

You could also consider using symbols (aka glyphs) in your subject lines, but ensure they are relevant to the context of the subject line, and also that your chosen icon renders correctly across different email clients.

Utilise different techniques to stand out in the inbox and draw attention to your content.

And don't forget to think about the format of your subject line – it is not best practice to write your subject line in all capitals (no one likes being SHOUTED AT!); using all caps or title case (where the first letter of each word is capitalised, except for certain small words) can also be seen by recipients as being a marketing email and may psychologically cause them to pass it over. Additionally, these two techniques can in some cases increase spam filter scores.

3. **Pre-header text** – use this area to back up your subject line and offer your main call-to-action.

Pre-header text is the first line of text that appears in an email before any other content. In many email clients, this text is shown underneath the subject line in the inbox.

When optimised and used to its full advantage, this can provide an additional space to supply more information to encourage subscribers to open the email. This area can also be used within your email to provide your main call-to-action – allowing subscribers to ascertain the main message and act immediately without even looking at the rest of your email. Some companies hide the pre-header text within the main design of their email (so that it still shows beneath the subject line in the inbox but not when the email is opened), however I would advise you to test this, as in my experience, this link is often clicked when a call-to-action link is provided and is another opportunity to place this within the top half of the email content.

Many companies miss this opportunity and do not optimise the text they put in this area, instead allowing *'view this email online'* text to be pulled through beneath the subject line. Although this type of messaging often needs to be at the top of your email, it should be secondary to optimised text that backs up your subject line.

For example:

eFocus Marketing ← FRIENDLY 'FROM' NAME

Learn how to create a highly successful email marketing strategy ← SUBJECT LINE

Read our latest blog post now! ← PRE-HEADER TEXT

Make sure you are optimising all three of these areas to stand out in the inbox.

In Gmail specifically, there is currently one other way you can stand out in the inbox – using 'Actions' and 'Highlights'.

Actions are buttons shown in the inbox that enable subscribers to interact with your product or service right inside Gmail. For example, when they receive an invitation to an event, they may be presented with the option to RSVP interactively from right inside the invitation. When they receive a notification that a magazine subscription is about to expire, they may be presented with the option to renew it right from the notification. In-App Actions are handled in place, inside Gmail and Inbox, without sending the user to any other website; these include One-Click Actions, Reviews and RSVP Actions.

Highlights take key information and actions from an email and display them as easy-to-see 'chips' in the inbox. For example, when a user receives a confirmation for a flight reservation, a chip may appear in their inbox with a summary of the trip and a link to check in. When they receive a receipt for an order, another chip may show an image of the purchase and even the expected delivery date.

You can find out more about this functionality here:
developers.google.com/gmail/markup/actions/actions-overview

Designing Your Emails for Engagement

When designing the layout of your email, it's important to consider the placement of key elements such as call-to-action buttons and different types of content, in order to encourage engagement and ensure that important information is clearly displayed.

This layout will be adapted to accommodate your design elements (whether you have an 's' shape design that leads from one side of the email to another, a 1:2 column-based layout or any other) but the main sections you will include remain the same.

So, thinking about the anatomy of a great email, we can divide the layout into 10 main sections:

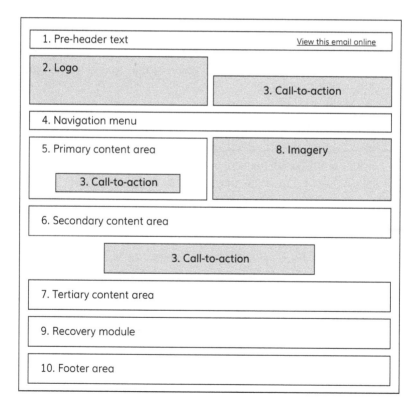

1. **Pre-header text**

   Add a pre-header summary (before the link to view online) that backs up your subject line, highlights your key message, and includes your main call-to-action link.

2. **Logo and other brand elements**

   Include clear branding in all of your email designs – this includes your logo, brand colours, fonts, style, and tone of voice, so that your messages are easily recognisable and recipients trust that the message is from you.

3. **Call-to-action buttons**

   As well as in your pre-header text, you should also aim to have your main call-to-action featured in the preview pane area of your email, as well as repeated throughout the content. This means that the subscriber doesn't need to scroll down further to find it when they want to take an action.

4. **Navigation menu**

   Include a navigation menu at the top of your email to offer functional links as well as to guide subscribers to key areas of your website, even if they aren't interested in the particular message or offer they have received.

   This should be a slimmed-down version of your main website navigation, offering 3-5 main options only. When designing for a mobile device, consider how this menu will display: whether it will stack, or become a hamburger menu that can be clicked on to reveal the links and if the options available need to be further reduced or hidden in this case.

5. Primary content area

This is where your main message and call-to-action will appear in your email. Some emails will only contain a primary content area with a single focus, others will have multiple areas of focus.

Think about an inverted triangle when designing your content; lead people from your headline, to your main message and down to your call-to-action button.

Especially in this area, ensure that even without going any further down your message, the main benefits of your offering and call-to-action can be seen and acted upon.

ATTENTION-GRABBING HEADLINE

Main Message

Key Points

**CTA
Button**

6. Secondary content area
7. Tertiary content area

These areas can be used where necessary to expand the content and offer additional information or showcase specific products, a selection of blog posts or links to specific areas of your website such as featured categories, for example.

8. Imagery
Many email clients (either due to default settings or personal preference) will block images automatically in emails (for example, many versions of Outlook), leading to 'broken' looking messages.

In some cases, where important information has been placed within images in the email design, this will also lead to an inability to understand what the message is advertising and how to take an action – possibly decreasing engagement as a result.

Even on mobile devices where images are usually enabled by default, there are times when data coverage is inconsistent or slow (for example on public transport) and images fail to load properly.

Therefore, it's important to optimise your email creatives for viewing with images turned off to ensure that the main message and call-to-action can still be seen and acted upon in this case.

Your imagery should back up your copy, not contain your main message.

It is also important to ensure you have used and optimised your 'ALT text' - when images are turned off or disabled, text populated in the ALT attribute (which is short for alternative text) often renders in place of the image.

It should however be noted that Outlook 2000, 2003, 2007, 2010, and 2013 preface ALT text with a lengthy security message, meaning that ALT text in these email clients only appears at the very end of Outlook's security warning – which most likely will then not be read.

Additionally, 'styled' ALT text (font, colour, size and weight attributes applied to this text) being displayed depends on which browser is being used to view the email within your webmail provider. For example, if you are using Chrome or Firefox to view your mailbox provider account (for example, Gmail), then styled ALT text will render; however, if you are using Internet Explorer to view these, font size, style and weight attribute wont display – although font type will.

9. Recovery module

This is a 'slimmed-down' version of your main site navigation that acts as a backup to your content, but can contain more options than your navigation bar at the top of your email.

It's another opportunity to continue the journey for the subscriber past the email. For example, if they scroll down your email and don't find anything that catches their interest, links to key categories on your site can encourage them to continue browsing and may highlight products/services they didn't know you offered.

10. Footer area

The footer area in your email should display a number of elements including:

o **a valid postal address** – it is a legal requirement in many countries to clearly show your identity, and allow people to write to you and request to be unsubscribed (if they so choose).

o **unsubscribe link** – every email needs an unsubscribe link (i.e. a link that when clicked, registers the unsubscribe action, and takes the recipient through to a landing page that confirms this and ideally offers other options such as connecting on social media, or re-subscribing but with a different set of preferences etc.).

o **link to a preference centre** – if you have a preference centre, include a link alongside your unsubscribe link to give subscribers another option, and allow them to tailor their communications from you, rather than unsubscribing completely.

o **a reminder of how the subscriber signed up** – a simple sentence that lets people know how and when they signed up can be helpful to reinforce your relationship in their mind, and avoid complaints stemming from people not remembering their previous interactions with you.

o **any terms and conditions** – if you're running an offer for example, include any specific terms and conditions in the email to avoid any confusion.

o **a link to your privacy policy** – in the interests of transparency, including a link to your privacy policy allows subscribers to find out more about how you treat their data.

Optimising Your Preview Pane Area

The preview pane is the top section of your email that is visible when someone previews it in their email client, but doesn't open it fully to read it. For example:

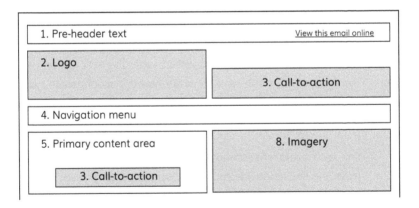

By optimising this area to include your main message (including an attention-grabbing headline, main message and call-to-action) you allow the reader to quickly understand and easily act, without scrolling through the rest of your email.

Enhancing Your Email Design

When it comes to designing your emails to encourage engagement, focus on enhancing these four main areas:

1. Design cues

Use your design to draw attention down to your main call-to-action and ensure you space out your content to make it easy to read. Design cues use colour, shapes and movement to draw the subscriber's attention to important information; for example, arrows pointing down to a call-to-action, or the inverted triangle design we talked about in the last section.

2. Typography

Your typography is a big part of directing the subscriber to the key pieces of information in your email, including your headlines, sub-headings, body copy and call-to-action text. The size, font and colours you use should represent your brand, but also differentiate between these different sections of your content.

3. Imagery

Imagery used in emails should support your main message, but not be the only way it is displayed. Remember, many email clients block images by default, so if the key message is added as an image, this will be lost completely if they are disabled.

Also consider the image size in terms of their width and height (i.e. make sure they fit into your email template), but also the weight within the email coding. Each character of code and image displayed within an email carries a weight that contributes to the overall email file size. If the email code or individual images are too heavy, it will be slow to load and can impact deliverability – aim to keep your email under 100kb.

4. Call-to-action buttons

Your call-to-action button has a vital role to play in your email design. It must be visible, eye catching, benefit-driven, tell the subscriber what will happen next and, of course, be actionable.

Keep these tips in mind when it comes to creating the perfect call-to-action that is easy to find and act on:

o **Make it bullet-proof and repeat it**
This is a type of button that is created in your HTML code as text, but is surrounded by background colours and images (to create curved corner effects, for example). When images are turned off, your 'button' is still shown (just minus the curved corners), ensuring it is still actionable.

Repeat your call-to-action at least once above the fold and at least once below the fold; have a mixture of text-based call-to-action links and bullet-proof buttons throughout your email to allow multiple opportunities to easily take the desired action.

o **Use colours**
Make your button stand out in your email design. For example, consider adding in buttons that are a contrasting colour to the background they are on and the colours that surround them, to make more of an impact.

For example, yellow and orange are opposite blue on the colour wheel so if this is your main brand colour, these could offer the most contrast.

o **Make the wording you use on your buttons benefit-driven, actionable and (if possible) personalised**
Think about the wording you use on your call-to-action text and how you can ensure that the main benefit to the subscriber is clearly stated and gives a clear and direct command of what to do. For example, 'Save 10% and buy now!', 'Join free for a month' or 'Secure your spot on the webinar now'.

You could also consider using some personalisation in your call-to-action to increase click rate. For example, 'Order [product name] now'.

o **Don't overwhelm the reader with too many options**
You should absolutely repeat your call-to-action multiple times throughout your email copy to give the subscriber numerous chances to act, but throwing in lots of different ones will simply confuse them and most likely lead to a decrease in engagement as they become overwhelmed with the options.

If you're asking people to do too many different things (like follow you on social media, links to blog posts, multiple products and product categories to explore, etc.), then you're likely overshadowing your main goal with lots of other little goals. Focus on the main goal for your email, and then use your call-to-action buttons to drive people through to that specific action.

Design to Capture Your Subscriber's Attention

Your design needs to capture the subscriber's attention and keep it long enough to direct them to your call-to-action. Here are some additional key design tips to keep in mind:

- Keep your email no more than 600–640 pixels wide so it's easy to read on small screens and within preview windows.

- Video and animated GIFs are now more feasible to use in email, thanks to advancements in technology. Consider how you can use these elements within your email to bring your content to life.

- Use colour, contrast and white space to draw attention to key conversion elements, for example, your call-to-action.

- Keep your design clear and uncluttered – remove distracting features.

- Split test design options to see which yield the highest conversion rates.

- People don't read emails – they scan them. Keep your email copy short and to the point and avoid long paragraphs and long sentences.

  o Break up text and emphasise key parts of the copy by using headings, bold font or bullet points.

  o Leave plenty of white space – large margins and line heights to make it easy to read.

- HTML and plain text versions

  Most emails are built using HTML code, the same code used to create websites. However, there are some essential differences in the way HTML can be used in an email versus a web page – the way your email looks to the recipient depends on the browser and/or email application they use, as well as on your design and coding. Email coding is a lot more limited than that used on a website and so the design needs to be created accordingly.

HTML emails contain images, stylised text, colours and links behind text.

In comparison, plain text versions are not built in this way and do not include any of these elements – they are simply text (for example, links are shown as the full links, rather than behind words which can be clicked on).

Both of these types of email are important to your sends. Most companies will use HTML emails (even if they don't include images etc. and have a simple looking email, they will still want to use stylised text including a specific font and bold keywords for example), although some may choose to have their main email as plain text.

When using an HTML email as your main creative, it's important to remember that not all receiving email clients will be able to handle this format (such as Apple Watch devices) and so a backup plain text version should always be created and sent alongside your HTML.

Where the HTML can be displayed, this will be shown, and the plain text version will effectively disappear. Where it can't be shown, the plain text version will display; this is often the case when emails are delivered to the spam folder, for example.

- Optimise for engagement on mobile devices.

With well over 50% of subscribers opening their email on a mobile device for many businesses, it is important to ensure your design is optimised to encourage engagement across the different ways that subscribers may view your emails.

Mobile users get a narrow single-column layout with large, touch-friendly buttons; desktop users get a wider layout with larger images and multiple columns.

Using various techniques, an email template can be optimised to allow for the best experience and easiest engagement on a mobile device. These include:

o a scalable template – a template made of just one design that is readable and clickable no matter which size device it is being read on

o a responsive template – a template created using Cascading Style Sheets (CSS) and media queries that renders different layouts depending on the size of the screen it is being viewed on

o using adaptive design – a template using static layouts based on breakpoints, which don't change once they're loaded.

Templates vs. Individually Designed Emails

Having distinct templates for different types of email is what most marketers would consider as sustainable and practical email design.

You may be under great pressure to get your campaigns sent, but without the ability to code, you are limited by the capabilities of your ESP's in-built editor, or what your designers have previously created. The alternative is having to rely on resources to create a new design for each email you want to send – a time-consuming process!

A modular email design allows you to keep brand consistency, whilst having the flexibility to adapt your email design on the fly for different purposes.

It is a skeleton that can be used to create any type of email from a set of different content blocks within your ESP's editor. This is particularly useful to ensure branding is consistent while the layout of alternate email types (newsletters, promotions, adverts for different product categories and so on) can be differentiated.

It's a bit like creating your email template with Lego bricks. Using the same set of blocks, you can build different structures, but within defined limits (keeping to certain colours, fonts, image sizes etc.), ensuring your designs are consistent and recognisable as part of your brand.

This is particularly helpful when needing to build multiple manual campaigns and wanting to cut out the need for a new design to be created as part of your process each time (consider this when reviewing and optimising your email design process in Chapter 2.8).

However, in some cases, such as automated campaigns which are more static (although of course these types of campaigns should still be reviewed, renewed and tested periodically to ensure they are optimised), a specific design, rather than one which can be regularly adapted on the fly, may be better suited.

These static templates are built and only changeable within that specific structure, or by altering the base HTML code – requiring a designer and developer to work on them and make changes.

CLIENT CASE STUDY

Client Type: Mobile networking provider

Objective: Increase conversion rate to enquiry.

Situation

The client was a supplier of third-party internet services (mobile networking) to exhibitors at events and trade shows in the USA. To make new prospects aware of their services, they had been sending a series of five emails to purchased lists of people exhibiting at upcoming events in a text-only format.

Challenges

The main challenge was to increase the engagement with these campaigns and, therefore, the revenue generated.

Other key challenges included:

- creating communications that are valuable to both the company and the recipients
- getting the message and timing right for each customer segment within the database
- encouraging subscribers to use and purchase them over competitors and internal venue providers.

<u>Solution</u>

eFocus Marketing conducted a full email template review of all five creatives currently being sent by the client. Through analysis of over 15 key creative best practice elements and the delivery of personalised recommendations in a comprehensive report alongside wireframe examples, we were able to pinpoint exact areas that could be optimised and improved to increase performance.

In performing this report, we suggested key recommendations such as:

- switching from a text-only to HTML-based template to allow for increased branding to build trust with prospects
- addition of increased information about the company and the services provided to educate the subscriber through the email series, leading to a sale
- optimisation of various creative elements such as the inclusion of a pre-header, increased calls-to-action through the content and subject line amendments
- recommendations around testing creative elements as well as the timing of the emails in the series.

Since implementing the recommended changes, the client has seen their conversions increase by 23%, unsubscribes decrease by 56% and spam complaints decrease by 69%, showing a more positive, responsive audience.

 # TAKE ACTION

- Conduct an official template review:

    1. Download your template review checklist.
    2. Choose one of your email templates to focus on.
    3. Work through each section of your template, scoring each accordingly.

- Once you have completed your review, look at the areas that you scored the lowest on or didn't have included in your template. List all the ways you could improve your template.

- Thinking about your current designs, consider whether you need to:

    o tweak them to make improvements
    o get a new design created to bring it more in line with brand guidelines, make it easier to interact with, or simply to bring it up-to-date
    o create additional modules that can be used within your template for different needs
    o change the type of email template you're using; is what you currently have best suited to each email type you send? For example, are you using a modular design, or a static template?

Remember to test any new designs against your current design to ensure positive engagement is increased by your changes.

You can download your template review checklist here: www.etelligencebook.com/members/step2/design/

2.6
Results Tracking

We've already discussed the results you are most likely already tracking (or should be) when it comes to your email marketing. But results are often affected by other factors outside of email such as the landing pages you are driving people to. It is possible to have a great email, but if the landing page falls down, people will not convert.

Optimise the way in which you look at your results by thinking past the email and considering the whole journey the customer takes – from opening an email to conversion. Analyse the website metrics you have available and consider how the pages your subscribers are being driven to could be further optimised to increase conversion.

Also, consider which pages you are actually taking people to from your email and make sure they are as specific as possible. For example, if you are advertising a certain product (or have an image of one) within your email content, ensure that when a subscriber clicks on it they are taken to that product and not a general category page.

You should also ensure that the pages you link to are present and helpful. For example, if you are advertising a product on sale, if possible add a message to the page and other related products, so that when that product has sold out or is no longer available you ensure that the journey is not broken (by a 404-page error for example).

Attribution Modelling

Many companies struggle when it comes to calculating the Return-on-Investment (ROI) of their email marketing campaigns as they cannot accurately track sales back to an individual email and campaign series, especially when other marketing channels are in the mix.

Attribution modelling refers to the rule, or set of rules, that determines how credit for sales and conversions is assigned to each touchpoint. The most commonly used attribution model is **'Last click'** – where 100% of the credit is attributed to the final touchpoint that immediately preceded the sale or conversion.

Other models that you could consider using include:

- **First click** – 100% credit to touchpoint that initiate conversion paths.

- **Last non-direct click** – similar to Last Click, except for cases when the Last Click is a direct visit. In such cases, this model finds the latest click that isn't a direct visit and attributes 100% of the revenue to that channel instead.

- **Linear** – every step of the customer journey is equally responsible; every touchpoint gets credit for an equal portion of the revenue a customer spends. For example, in a customer journey where the consumer had five interactions, each will be credited with 20% of the revenue from that customer.

- **Positional** – combining aspects of the First Click, Last Click and Linear models. The first touchpoint and the last touchpoint are worth X% each (whatever percentage you decide), and all the other touchpoints in between have the remaining percentage divided evenly among them.

- **Time decay** – the closer (in terms of time) a touchpoint is to the conversion, the more influence that touchpoint had on the customer decision and therefore it gets the most credit.

- **Position-based** – 40% credit is assigned to both the first and the last interaction, and the remaining 20% credit is distributed evenly to the middle interactions.

✎ TAKE ACTION

- Start by looking at which emails create high click-through rates, but low conversion rates and vice versa.

  Use a system such as Google Analytics, and analyse the performance of your landing pages. Gain insights around bounce rates, exit rates, click-through rates, dwell time, conversion rates etc.

  Consider improvements you could make to the pages you are linking to from your email – either to optimise the pages themselves, or link to alternate pages that would be more helpful or relevant to the subscriber in that case.

- Consider the type of attribution model you use within your company (if any). What are the restrictions you have on calculating this? Could you be using a more robust model?

2.7
Testing Strategy

Testing is critical to allow you to continuously learn and inform your overall strategy, content development, image selection, and design of your campaigns, in order to improve and maximise your results.

Most elements are really easy to test and there is a multitude of technology out there to help you. But not many people bother – either because they are unsure how to, don't know what technology to use, think that it will be too time-consuming or have never seen good results from tests they have run previously.

Tweak – Test – Optimise – Repeat
= Results

Every test you run is a learning opportunity. Not just for that individual email, but for every campaign you're planning going forward; it is important to ensure you use this learning in future sends (and even across other marketing channels).

Frequently testing your campaigns and strategy will allow you to increase your results; but remember, you may see decreases in your results on some of the tests you run... and that's OK!

It's a constant cycle to improve your results.

Kate's 5-Step Method for Implementing Meaningful Tests

In order to create a testing strategy that gives you solid learnings that can be used in future campaigns, it is important to conduct meaningful tests. The way in which you do this is to know what you are testing, why and what determines a winning result.

Here is my five-step method to help you do this:

Step 1 – Choose your test element and form a hypothesis

Before you start testing you need to know WHY you are running the test and what you THINK the outcome will be so that you have something to measure against.

Without knowing what you want to test and why you are doing it, you are not allowing yourself to generate a result and learning that can be used in future campaigns.

Choose one specific test that you want to run and, rather than using a 'we like this over this' testing approach, instead opt for a structured hypothesis.

For example, your hypothesis may be:

> *'We think that shorter subject lines (under 35 characters) will create more positive engagement than longer subject lines (over 35 characters), because 85% of our audience open our emails on a mobile device and this is the length at which subject lines commonly wrap.'*

Rather than 'We like this subject line over this subject line' which has no discernible difference that could be used going forward beyond that specific email and test.

The more specific you are with your hypothesis, the better and more meaningful the results you will receive.

Where Will You Start?

Every element of your campaign can be tested so how do you decide where to start? Take a look at your current results – where do you think you can make the most impact? Are your open rates low? Click rates non-existent? Conversion rates decreasing?

Whichever it is, start there and select the element that can help you make the most impact to that statistic.

For example:

Test element	Most likely to have an impact on
Subject line	Open rate
Call-to-action: colour/ placement/wording	Click-through rate
Type of offer shown	Click-through rate/conversion rate

Step 2 - Choose your KPIs (Key Performance Indicators)

KPIs are the metrics used to monitor and inform you if the test has been successful.

For example, these could include:

- opens
- clicks
- click-to-open rate
- conversion rate
- AOV
- total revenue
- ROI

For each test, you need to choose which is the most appropriate metric (or combination of metrics) to determine your winning version.

So, to expand on Step 1, your hypothesis should also include:

'We will measure engagement for this test by monitoring open and click rates – if both increase, or even if open rate decreases but click rate increases, we will deem this version the winner of the test.'

Step 3 – Confirm your testing requirements and timings

This includes the date of the test send as well as any follow-up sends to prove the result.

Depending on the type of test and the hypothesis, you may need to consider running your test over multiple campaigns/weeks to ensure that the results you are seeing are valid.

You will also need to decide on any segments you need to create, additional analytics to be monitored, new images that need to be created or copy to be written etc. in order to perform the test. This can then be briefed to other teams within your business to gather the assets needed to allow you to run the test.

Versions

The main element to decide is what are the different versions you will use to test – for example, if you are testing your call-to-action button colour, you may already be using a green button (this is your control version that you continue to run and measure all other tests against to see if the changes have a positive or negative impact), and you want to test to see if a blue, red or orange button colour has a better click rate – these are your test versions.

Ensuring Statistical Significance

'Statistical significance is the likelihood that the difference in conversion rates between a given variation and the baseline is not due to random chance.'
(Source: Optimizely)[9]

Basically, this means that the results of the tests you run are actually true and not just a coincidence; they are reliable and you can use these results as you move forward and make changes to your email programme based on these results.

Your statistical significance is created through the use of two main variables:

Your sample size: when you run a test, you're taking a sample of your list – a sample group.

The larger your sample size, the more confident you can be in the result of the experiment (this should be a randomised sample). If you don't send each test segment to enough contacts, you won't be able to count on your results being statistically significant.

Your minimum effect size: this is the minimum change in results between the sample sets that you would like to see. For example, if you chose 30% and your baseline conversion was 10%, one of your variations would need at least 13% to secure a statistically significant result. The smaller the effect size, the more emails you'll need to send to be sure of the result.

You also need to decide your **statistical significance level** – this reflects your risk tolerance and confidence level.

For example, if you run an A/B split test with a significance level of 95%, this means that if you determine a winner, you can be 95% confident that the observed results are real and not an error caused by randomness. It also means there is a 5% chance that you could be wrong.

In order to calculate statistical significance, the best way is to simply search online for a 'statistical significance calculator' and you'll find lots of resources to help you find the right sample size for your campaigns.

Step 4 – Perform your test
When running your test, remember:

- Only test one element at a time (when using A/B split testing – multivariate testing of course means multiple combinations of the same elements) so that you always know what made the difference to your results.

- Test your hypothesis at least three times before you arrive at a final conclusion – one test is not enough to give you a reliable result.

- Always check that your result is statistically significant.

- Don't forget, you should also be testing your sign-up forms and landing pages too!

Step 5 – Record and analyse your results

It's really important to make sure you look at all of your statistics together after running a test and before deciding a winner, and not just one metric in isolation, in order to have a true view of how the test performed.

Use the tab within your 'Split Test Year Planner' kit (download it here – www.etelligencebook.com/members/step2/testing/) to record your tests and the results achieved so that you always have a record of what was tested, why, the results and how the learnings can be used going forward.

This can also be shared with other departments of the business so that everyone is on the same page and using the learnings – you could also adapt the spreadsheet to be used for PPC (Pay per Click advertising campaigns), social media and other marketing tests!

✒ TAKE ACTION

- Create a testing strategy and systematically work through different hypotheses to find out what works best for your audience.

  Think about:

  o What do we want to improve?
  o What can we change to generate opportunities for improvement?
  o Are the variations different enough?
  o Can we re-use the resulting information in other campaigns, or across other marketing channels?

- Use **Kate's 5-Step Method for Implementing Meaningful Tests**

You can download your split test planning kit here:
www.etelligencebook.com/members/step2/testing/

2.8

Technology and Processes

Once you know what you most like and dislike about your current technology, as well as your future requirements, you need to decide whether you are happy to stay with the providers you currently have, or if you need to start researching other competitors on the market and add-on systems.

The systems you use shouldn't just provide a function, but also help you to save time and improve your processes.

Don't just consider ESPs and marketing automation platforms, but also other third-party technologies that can provide bolt-on services to help you get more from your time and efforts – whether to improve your design, speed up and make your QA process more robust, or increase your ability to personalise your communications through AI/Machine Learning, for example.

In any areas you are considering adding new technology, once you have narrowed your list of possible providers down to the vendors that meet your specific criteria, choose your top three (to begin with) and sign up for free trials (if available) or schedule a demo with each.

- Ask questions to ensure the platform meets your needs and really use this time to evaluate the features, functionality and ease of use thoroughly.

- Work through key tasks (in the case of an ESP or marketing automation platform, this could include tasks such as importing exporting data, creating segments, editing emails and reviewing results).

- Call customer services to test response times.

- Make sure that all potential internal users are on the demo call so that they can also get a feel for the system.

- Find out the development plan for the platform over the coming 12 months and what additional features and functionality are likely to be updated/added.

You are looking to find not only the platform's strengths, but also its weaknesses; and then to decide if these are weaknesses that you can live with or affect elements that are vital to your business.

This self-assessment is a critical step to finding the right platform for your current and future business needs. Be brutally honest and you'll end up choosing a platform that works for your business and brings you the ability to achieve amazing results from your campaigns.

Choose the solution that best suits your needs, while also allowing for strategic give and take.

Ask for other opinions

Speaking to other companies and people within their teams, who are actually using the systems you are considering on a day-to-day basis, is a great way to find out their experience of using the platform and discover any strengths and weaknesses they have found.

Many platforms will happily supply details of other customers who are using the platform (although this may be biased towards happy customers); alternatively, look to your own network for anyone who is using/has used the systems you're considering recently and ask them questions such as:

- Has there been any downtime?
- Are there any problems they are having with the system?

- What are their favourite features?
- Do they find it easy to use?
- How do they find their customer service support? Are they responsive?
- Did you migrate to this platform from another? If so, how was the conversion process?
- Why did you choose to use this platform over others on the market?
- How long did the system take to get up and running? Did you receive the level of support you needed during this time? How is the selection of help resources available?
- Has this platform lived up to your expectations?
- Are you pleased with any integrations you have in place with this platform?
- Were there any surprises that you wish you'd known about beforehand?
- What is the most useful, actionable (favourite) part of the platform?
- What do you wish they did differently/had as a feature that they don't?
- Why would you recommend this platform?

Businesses can also use these kinds of questions to create a Request for Proposals (RFP) when seeking tenders or when comparing bids in a pitch from different email marketing service or marketing automation providers.

Start the migration process

After thoroughly evaluating your shortlist of systems, it is time to make a decision as to the platform you want to employ. This decision will of course also feature your budget requirements, but don't forget to also look for a system that will:

- grow with your business
- offer comprehensive reporting
- provide technological capabilities that match your needs

- be easy to use
- give great support

When moving from one sending platform to another don't forget to move all of your current assets (such as images, templates and data), record all historical statistics, and ensure that (if you're using dedicated IPs) you have a proper IP warm-up plan in place (we discuss this activity later in Chapter 5.2).

 **TAKE ACTION**

In each of the three areas we looked at in Chapter 1.8, consider how you could improve the technology you are using or streamline the processes you currently have in place.

1. The technology you're using

- Do you need to start thinking about researching other technology to replace your current systems or add on to them?

- Create an RFP if needed/research and contact companies to evaluate.

- Set up a demo/test of your top three systems and put it through its paces!

- Choose a system that best meets your needs both now, and in the future and start your migration/integration.

- Refer to the following checklist as a starting point when migrating from one ESP or marketing automation platform to another.

Element	Completed
Database exported (including all activity data and any tags etc. associated with each record)	
Suppression list exported; a list of anyone who has been marked as non-contactable due to an unsubscribe request, failed delivery (hard/ soft bounce), complaint removal or for any other reason	

Element	Completed
Exported all creatives (Email: HTML and Text-only emails/SMS etc.); templates as well as old designs you may want to refer back to: • Manually sent emails • Automated campaigns • SMS templates • Social media post templates	
Any images (that are not saved externally already) have been exported from the platform image library	
You've made a note of any rules associated with automated email campaigns	
Results data for previous campaign sends exported for future reference	
Any sign-up form or landing page templates have been saved/exported	

You can download a copy of this checklist here:

www.etelligencebook.com/members/step2/technology/

2. Your email development process

Think about how you could accelerate your email creation and testing processes – and to keep error rates close to zero:

• Could you implement a modular email design?

• Could you implement additional third-party technology – this could allow you to automate large portions of your pre-send testing efforts to reduce overall testing times (such as reviewing designs in all popular email clients and devices to make sure they render properly and as they should everywhere, without having to manually check a large set of test accounts on individual devices).

- Analyse which email environments matter most to your audience, so that your team can focus their optimisation efforts on the most critical email clients and spend less time on those that aren't relevant to the client's subscriber base.

3. **Your QA (quality assurance) process**

- How could you streamline your QA process while maintaining low error rates?

- Develop your own internal checklist to monitor elements that are important to your designs and business needs.

CASE STUDY

Client Type: Retail

Objective: To change how they work – making the production process smarter and increasing revenue generated from the channel.

Situation

You'll know Debenhams as a cornerstone of the British high street, but might not be aware that email is the cornerstone of their marketing strategy. It is the highest performing channel and in 2018 helped drive a significant part of online revenue.

There are some things that are done for almost every campaign – content changes subtly depending on whether the customer is a member of Beauty Club or Debenhams' loyalty scheme. Plus, we often change content depending on your local store, and we also create versions of our email campaigns with Euro pricing for Ireland.

Challenges

Historically, the email team were working hard, often working late, to get the day-to-day done. They were producing around 5 emails a week, with an average lead time of 2 weeks per email, so at any one time there were at least 10 email campaigns being made.

There were lots of stakeholders in the process, and the emails were being created by an agency, some of which were outsourced, causing time-zone conflicts. As a result, it often took over 100 email exchanges to create one email campaign and we couldn't influence any last-minute changes to react to business needs. The team was capable, but had very little time left to step back and improve their process or email execution – or even work on longer term strategy.

Because they were focused on getting campaigns done, the team were often working on their own, with a siloed approach. That could sometimes lead to an inconsistent experience for the customer and make them unreactive to the business.

The Solution

Since we moved to Taxi, we've been able to create email campaigns ourselves with a real collaborative approach internally between the CRM and Design teams. We have a couple of master templates set up in Taxi, which have all the building blocks we need, as well as dynamic rules set up for our own customer data. Our marketers drag and drop modules to decide the overall layout, then they add the key products and categories that we know will drive customer interaction and conversion. Once we're happy with the layout, our copywriting team goes into the tool to write the content to fit. It's much more collaborative internally.

The content of our email has improved a lot, because we've been able to put the job of writing straight into the hands of people who know about fashion and our products and, most importantly, design mobile-first (the majority of engagement is done through mobile devices, so we have to make sure our design takes into account our customers' viewing habits). It's great that we were able to do this, whilst being able to keep our existing sending platform.

We've also been able to add to our master templates and make changes as we go along, as our approach to content changes over time and the team at Taxi have been really flexible.

On average, how long does it take to create an email campaign with Taxi?

We now turn around emails much quicker. We still keep our two-week lead times to allow for focus on campaigns and long-term strategy, something we couldn't consider before. But we can now also turn them around within the same day if we need to react to a business need.

Usually, a long turnaround time is great for email marketers. But in our case, it meant there was more risk of prices changing or products going out of stock. In the old world, this meant delays to campaigns, and rush fees getting the agency to make updates. Now, if the price does ever change, the teams can make updates quickly themselves.

How has the dynamic of the team changed?

We now have a larger, stronger team who work closely with content editors and designers who are committed to our brand. As well as creating email campaigns ourselves, we also spend more time looking at our data strategy, including things like personalisation, segmentation and dynamic content. The team is a lot happier, because they have much more control over their work and they see the results coming through.

What successes have you seen from the new way of working?
Because email is now so much easier to make, we've been able to try out new ideas quickly. It's enabled us to make incremental changes, that all add up to much better email over time.

A while ago, we worked with the Taxi team to improve the analytics of our email campaigns. Now every link that our team adds to an email has analytics code added automatically, with the necessary campaign identifiers sent straight to our attribution team. It's meant we've been much more able to prove the value of email to the rest of the business and show which campaigns are working, especially when we're A/B testing creative or targeting.

Since using Taxi, we've been able to try out deeper levels of segmentation and personalised content.

How has Taxi helped you achieve your KPIs?
As an eCommerce and high street retailer, naturally one of our strongest KPIs is revenue.

Over the last couple of years, we've been able to increase the revenue generated from email significantly. In addition, we've been able to make the money we do spend on email work much harder – primarily by making the team much more effective.

By being able to demonstrate the revenue we generate, we've made the email team the superstars of the marketing department!

CHAPTER 3

FILL IN
Your Gaps

Now you have a clear idea of what you currently have and are well on the way to making improvements, it's time to evaluate how you can extend your strategy and have even more of an impact on your results. This involves finding the gaps in your current plans and filling them in with new, highly targeted and relevant campaigns.

It is important to have completed the last two sections before trying to add any new campaigns so that there are no unnecessary (and potentially irritating) overlaps and so that you know where the most value can be added in the quickest and easiest way from the start.

Try evaluating your campaigns on a scale to help you decide which to work on first – those that are easiest for your organisation to implement, or that will have the most impact (those with the highest score should be implemented first).

Campaign description	Ease of implementation (1-10 – 10 being easiest to implement)	Potential impact (1-10 – 10 being highest impact)	Total score

See Appendix 6 on page 306 for an example.

You can download a copy of this as a worksheet here:
www.etelligencebook.com/members/step3/evaluationscale/

3.1
Optimising Your Email Marketing Strategy

To optimise and add to your email marketing strategy and improve campaign results, you need to have a clearly defined set of objectives by which to measure performance and inform future strategies and tactics being implemented. This will ensure that new ideas are always in line with what you want to achieve.

An effective email marketing strategy takes into consideration who your target customers are, their preferences, as well as your products/ services and industry, to determine which email campaigns will be most effective.

Start with a vision of what you are trying to achieve and be extremely clear as to the purposes of your email marketing activity – this will help you decide what you need to implement to get you there.

Setting Your Objectives

At a top level, you will have your overarching business objectives. These set out what you want to achieve across your whole business such as increasing sales, informing the target audience, or increasing overall probability.

Marketing objectives then connect these high-level objectives and your day-to-day operations to detail what you want to achieve from your marketing activities. In this instance, measured in terms of reach, overall customer base, retention levels etc, for example.

Email marketing objectives are the specifics of your campaigns which, in this case, will include Key Performance Indicators (KPIs). Email can of course be used to support a range of high-level objectives, each of which can be supported by a corresponding KPI. For example:

Objective	Potential KPI
• Increase brand awareness	• Open rate, click-through rate, and open-to-click rate
• Increase sales revenue	• Click-to-purchase rate, conversion rate
• Increase profitability	• Cost per conversion/acquisition/purchase

Here are some examples of common financial and efficiency objectives:

- Financial objectives

  o Increase sales directly through email campaigns vs. indirectly by an increase in traffic to store, website or events, or referrals via phone/email orders.

  o Increase repeat business through greater customer awareness and customer-specific reward programmes.

  o Shorten the sales cycle by using email marketing to distribute key information more quickly and efficiently.

  o Lower costs through the use of automation and a reduced need to deliver information in print form.

- Efficiency objectives

  o Automate key tasks, therefore ensuring that these happen every time (for example, use autoresponders, and always direct customers to a particular website etc.).

  o Reduce time spent on administrative tasks (for example, encourage customers to update their own information, automate list management etc.).

  o Educate customers on your product/service and offer free tips and advice on how to make the most out of their purchase.

  o Obtain customer feedback through the use of surveys/polls and email behavioural data, to allow you to spot areas of weakness in your email marketing, or overall business activities that could be improved.

Using SMART Objectives

Creating SMART objectives is a great way to provide clear direction and targets that you need to meet within your marketing activities. For example, if you are looking to grow your email list, and you have set an objective of achieving growth of 5% over the next 12 months, this would be considered a SMART objective because it is:

- **Specific** – it is exact in terms of subscriber numbers.

- **Measurable** – it is associated with a concrete measure against which success can be assessed.

- **Achievable** – this cannot be determined absolutely from the example objective. However, it is likely that before setting this objective, the business would have assessed its ability to deliver this increase within the timescale set.

- **Realistic** – again this cannot be absolutely determined, but it may be assumed that before setting this objective, the business looked at resources in terms of promotional budget and sales force and determined that it could deliver against this objective.

- **Timed** – the window of a single year within which to deliver this objective.

Adopting SMART principles is a good start to the goal-setting process. In addition, the following guidelines are important:

- **Stay realistic** – although this is a key component of SMART, is your goal-setting truly realistic? It may be possible to add 2,000 new subscribers in a two-month period for example, but if the process of getting approval and setting up new systems takes seven weeks, is it realistic to achieve that goal in the one remaining week?

- **Break down your goals into time-blocks** – this is not quite the same as the T of SMART, which is about setting a deadline for achievement of an overall objective. This is more about using a timeline when planning and is closely related to being realistic. For example, if you need to generate 2,000 new subscribers in two months, how many do you need to achieve in one month? In two weeks? Where a complex conversion path is being followed to generate new customers for example, how many prospects do you need to gain in Week 1 in order to generate the target conversion rate by Week 4?

- **Relate objectives to ROI** – this is a measure of whether your activity is ultimately profitable or not. It is acceptable for some objectives, some of the time, not to generate a positive ROI. Where the majority of objectives are failing to do so, there may be a flaw in your overall business strategy, which needs to be addressed.

Once you have set your objectives, detail the specific strategies that will help you achieve them. For example:

Objective	Strategies
Increase repeat purchases by 10% compared with last year	1. Improve customer service through a targeted post-purchase automation series 2. Promote a customer loyalty programme 3. Offer a discount to make a repeat purchase 4. Send personalised, engaging email campaigns on a regular basis

Defining Your Tactics

Once you know WHAT you want to achieve, you can start to drill down on the tactics – what needs to happen to get you there. Tactics are the steps and actions you need to take to achieve an objective – the details of how you are going to get there, your day-to-day actions.

Now you can add this to your plan. For example:

Objective	Strategies	Tactics
Increase repeat purchases by 10% compared with last year	1. Improve customer service through a targeted post-purchase automation series. 2. Promote a customer loyalty programme. 3. Offer a discount to make a repeat purchase. 4. Send personalised, engaging email campaigns on a regular basis.	1. Implement a series of 5 emails post-purchase to show the customer how to make the most of the product they've purchased including tutorial videos and links to help articles. Also feature cross-sell products that complement the previous purchase. 2. Notify customers of loyalty scheme with an email within the post-purchase cycle of messaging. Remind the customer of this programme in all future messaging as well as the number of points they currently have and the rewards of the scheme. 3. Send an email with a discount code 30 days after first purchase made, if a second purchase hasn't already been made. 4. Use data collected on sign-up (known data) and purchase data to personalise product suggestions in all future emails.

By creating clear and actionable objectives, you can see what types of campaigns are missing from your current strategy that would help you to achieve them.

✎ TAKE ACTION

- Think about the objectives that already exist in your business and how you can use your email marketing campaigns to achieve them.

- Set SMART email marketing objectives.

- Match the tactics (specific action and campaigns) to these objectives – what is missing from your current strategy? For example, growing your email list – how will you do this? Or could you implement new manual/automated campaigns at different stages of the customer journey to help achieve specific objectives – we'll go into this further in the next section.

You can download a copy of this as a worksheet here: www.etelligencebook.com/members/step3/objectives/

3.2

Enhancing the Customer Journey

When adding to your strategy to help you meet your objectives, you need to understand what campaigns are going to best service your subscribers.

To do this, you should start by digging deeper into the customer journey to really understand their needs at each stage and how you can best serve them to help them move to the next.

The five stages of a typical customer journey include:

Acquisition & Discovery
Finding your brand

What are they searching for?
Create content that inspires/reduces their fears/captures their attention. Introduce your brand.

Reactivation
Encouraging inactive subscribers/purchasers

How can you encourage them to come back again and make another purchase from you, or re-engage with your email programme?

Research & Consideration
Discovering the right product/ service for their needs

What do they need to know to make a choice and purchase? FAQs/allay fears/get excited/why your brand?

Loyalty & Repeat Purchase
Encouraging them to buy again and become a fan

What will inspire loyalty?
Keep educating post-purchase – create VIPs.

Purchase & Experience
Making their purchase and post-purchase experience

Make the purchase experience as smooth and enjoyable as possible. Support customer services and help the customer.

To map this process and explore your prospects' needs at each stage, gather your teams together to conduct a customer journey workshop. During this session, follow these 3 steps.

Step 1 – what do your prospects need from you at each stage?

To assess the best type of campaigns and content to send in order to maximise engagement at each stage, ask yourself the following five questions:

1. **What tasks are they completing?** For example, are they searching on Google, scanning their social media feeds, or checking their emails for a new offer?

2. **What touchpoints are they interacting with to achieve these tasks?** For example, Google, Facebook, blogs, print ads in a specific magazine, train or tube ads, radio ads, price comparison sites etc.

These first two questions will tell you where best to target people with your messaging at each stage. Email marketing is the primary communication channel in most cases once a prospect has found your business and registered to receive marketing; therefore, mainly from Research and Consideration onwards.

3. **What are they trying to achieve?** For example, are they still in the early stages of researching, or do they specifically know what they are looking for? The types of keywords/phrases they are searching in Google can give you an idea of this, as can their behaviour on your website and the pages they are viewing. This will help you to create content that helps them to move forward and gain the answers they are looking for, as well as send emails based around specific actions they are taking to get this information to them at the right time.

4. **How do they feel at this stage in their journey?** For example, are they excited, scared, happy, nervous? They may not consciously know themselves how they are feeling but their behaviour will tell

you a lot – for example, the types of words they are using in their search terms. Knowing this will help you to target the tone of your content correctly.

5. **What questions are they looking to get answered?** For example, what does the prospect want to know about at this stage to help them move forward? Benefits? Features? Again, this helps you to create content to answer those questions for them quickly and easily.

Think about what content you already have/need to create to meet the needs you have identified above. You really need to understand that prospects are looking for different types of content at different stages of the customer journey and the decision-making process they are going through.

The specific topics of the content you send will then also depend on that individual subscriber – for example, blog content depending on the information they provided on sign-up or the products they have been viewing and blog posts that will give them inspiration in those areas. Or, if they were browsing womenswear, you could deliver inspiration of collated content on blog posts or blogger recommendations to move them towards specific products, for example.

Your job is to identify this content and serve it to them at the right time to assist in this process – this is where you can also start to identify new campaigns to implement within your strategy to create messaging that is highly relevant and engaging.

Gaining input from other areas of the business will help you to identify known content that you already possess, as well as key questions that potential customers ask before they move on to buy.

This process once again puts your customers at the heart of your strategy.

And don't forget to map each possible journey, for all stages of the lifecycle, for different customer personas as the answers to the above questions will differ in some places.

Step 2 – ascertain your organisation's current weaknesses at each stage

Once you've started to break down what customers are doing, asking and feeling at each stage, you need to consider where your organisation is currently letting subscribers down at each stage, by not providing the right information at the right time.

When you know the areas in which your prospects, and in this case your email subscribers, are being let down, you can create new content and campaigns to better serve them and meet their needs.

Step 3 – make sure you can identify prospects at each stage in order to correctly target them

If you don't know who you are talking to, how can you send the right information to them in a way that resonates with their situation, needs, wants and desires, in order to produce the best results?

Using the data you have, you can then identify different types of customers and their current position in their journey to better serve the right message to the right person at the right time.

The work you did in Chapters 1 and 2 will support you in identifying what this data is and how you can make it accessible within your business. In some cases, this may not be possible immediately or without much input from other areas of the business or development work.

But even so, it is vital you know what you need, in order to start to move your company in that direction – even if it takes many years to eventually get there! If you don't start today, this process will only be further delayed.

Using Lead Scoring to Identify Customers at Different Stages of Their Journey

When it comes to identifying where your individual customer personas are at in their customer journey in order to provide the right information at the right time, individual indicators such as browse behaviour can be used. However, if you want to take this a step further, lead scoring helps to bring together multiple actions in a layered format to see the larger connected picture of the actions being taken by an individual.

Lead scoring is a methodology used to rank prospects against a scale that represents the perceived value each lead represents to the business. It is often used by B2B companies but can be very useful for B2C companies to adopt as well.

Each action the prospect takes can be ranked with a certain number of points (numeric score) that denotes its importance in the customer journey and their propensity to buy. For example, someone downloading a free guide, reading blog posts or attending a webinar would receive a lower number of points than someone requesting a free trial, watching demo videos or viewing pricing/product pages.

The resulting score is then used to determine when a lead is 'sales ready' vs. a cold prospect, and those somewhere in between. Targeted marketing campaigns can then be sent to reflect this (or even pass the lead to a sales team to also follow up with in the case of many B2B companies).

*Marketers cited prioritized leads (74%) and improved
conversion rates (41%) as just some of the payoffs
to well executed lead scoring initiatives.*
*'Lead scoring helps companies predict where a buyer is in their
purchase journey. This enables companies to meet the buyer's
expectation by intelligently tailoring communications and
facilitating seamless hand-offs between marketing and sales.'*
(Source: Demand Gen Report's '2016 Lead Scoring Survey')[10]

There are many ways to break down the activities that prospects go through and to assign a relevant score to, so this is a task that should be undertaken with both marketing and sales input (for B2B) to ensure the right values are assigned to actions.

The details of your lead scoring system will be specific to your business and audience.

Implementing New Campaigns at Each Stage of the Customer Journey

Let's take a look at some examples of campaigns you may want to implement at each stage in a little more detail.

1. Acquisition and Discovery Stage

This stage is made up of the initial touchpoints with the user as they become a subscriber – for email marketing this is mainly focused around the sign-up form and the initial communications that are sent immediately following this action.

74.4% of consumers expect a welcome email when they subscribe.
(Source: BlueHornet, 2013)[11]

People that read at least one welcome message read more than 40% of their messages from the sending brand during the following 180 days.
(Source: Return Path, 2015)[12]

Welcome emails have 320% more revenue per email than other promotional emails.
(Source: Easy-SMTP, 2015)[13]

Once a new subscriber is on your email list, send an automated welcome and on-boarding series to lead prospects through the initial stages of the customer journey from acquisition, through to consideration and purchase.

Your aim with this series is to delight new subscribers and inspire them as to the range of products you offer, educate them on the services you provide, as well as lead them through to what they are most likely to purchase based on their behaviour and other data gathered since sign-up.

An automated welcome and on-boarding series is your first chance to communicate directly with a subscriber and welcome them to not only your email programme, but most importantly, your brand. It allows you an opportunity to start the relationship off on the right foot and begin to build a positive connection with them in the right way.

The welcome email is the first communication they will receive from you (unless you are using double opt-in to confirm the subscription, in which case this will technically be the second email they receive from you) following registration on your sign-up form.

Your welcome message should:

- welcome and thank them for subscribing
- reinforce expectations of what they have signed up for
- deliver the opt-in offer if applicable, such as a link to download/ discount code etc.
- provide any important information they need to be aware of
- provide tools/instructions for personal whitelisting (adding your sending domain to their address book)
- direct users to be able to change their preferences (where applicable).

The on-boarding series follows the initial welcome email and extends your opportunity to talk to the subscriber during the critical time period following this action when they are most likely to be engaged with your brand, usually the first 30 days after subscription.

Use this opportunity to initiate a positive brand experience, focus on educating the subscriber, and make the experience with the programme and your brand as positive and meaningful as possible. Content within this series of emails could include relevant information about your brand/products/services/key areas of your brand to explore.

In Chapter 2.4 I've given an example of a welcome and on-boarding email series plan that you could use as a starting point.

eF⊙CUS
Marketing

CLIENT CASE STUDY

Client Type: Homeware retailer

Objective: Create an optimised strategy for a structured welcome email series to on-board new subscribers and encourage the first sale.

Situation

This popular retailer was generating a significant number of new sign-ups, but were simply adding these new subscribers straight into the email programme with a single, non-optimised welcome email sent to introduce the subscriber to the brand.

Challenges

Not only was the original welcome email basic in nature and not optimised for conversion or to boost customer satisfaction, it also had issues with rendering in Gmail and the discount code offered did not work.

We also found that 55% of subscribers had not made a purchase, representing a significant opportunity to increase sales in the crucial period following sign-up.

Solution

eFocus Marketing undertook an email marketing strategy creation project to extend the single email to a series of five emails sent over two weeks post sign-up. Each of these emails also contained dynamic content sections which changed based on click behaviour with the previous emails in the series and website browse behaviour during that time, to personalise the content and ensure relevancy.

For example, if the subscriber had clicked on a specific category of product, or shown an interest in specific types of product, then the following emails would highlight relevant suggestions based on this behaviour.

On implementing these new additions and optimisation of the content, we saw open rates increase by up to 53% and click-through rates up 135% in comparison to the company's general campaigns; with open rates averaging 52% across the series, click-through rates 24% and click-to-open rates 45%. Revenue per email was also up 1278% and conversion rate 1178% in comparison to general campaigns.

In the six months following implementation, the series had also brought in £45,000+ in additional revenue.

2. Research and Consideration Stage

During this stage of the journey, you need to provide the subscriber with communications that help them to decide that you are the right company to purchase from, and that you have the right product/service to meet their needs and wants. They may not even know exactly what those are at this stage!

Take this opportunity to educate and inspire your subscribers and give them the information they need to make the right decision (this can be identified through your customer journey workshop for example, and the questions they are asking at this stage).

As previously mentioned, many of the campaigns you send will happen during this stage: informational newsletters, regular sales (including promotional) campaigns, and back-in-stock messages – all mailings that display your products/services to the customer in an enticing way.

Abandoned Action Emails

Depending on whether your business is B2B or B2C, there will be different abandon actions that may happen that trigger an automated communication encouraging the subscriber to take an action. For example, for B2C organisations, you may have an abandoned basket email encouraging the subscriber to come back and buy the products that have been left in their basket.

This is a fantastic email to implement if you don't have it in your strategy plans already, or to optimise if you are already running it as it is one of the highest revenue-earning campaigns in your arsenal. It is designed to pick up on people who have already been through 99% of the purchase process with you but have fallen at the last hurdle.

When creating this type of campaign, I suggest sending a series of three emails (testing the timing of each to see what is optimal for your audience between 1 hour and 5 days post-cart abandonment) and ensuring that you not only remind them of the items left in their basket, but also address some of the key reasons why they may not have completed the purchase. These may include:

- saving items to buy later
- still deciding if this is what they want
- wanted to confirm the item met their needs
- total cost was too high

I would also advise considering offering alternate purchase options in email two and three – if they haven't gone on to make the purchase by then, the original items they found may not have met their needs or they may not have found the perfect product for them.

For B2B organisations, you may have an abandoned form email triggered when someone completes the first stage of a form but does not go on to complete the process.

For both B2B and B2C organisations, you can implement abandoned browse emails; for B2C these will focus on inspiring subscribers to come back and continue to explore a category of products or specific type of product they were looking at, and to make a purchase.

Whereas for B2B, these would suggest other related blog posts or content they may like, based on what they have already looked at, or to encourage them towards more product information if they have shown behaviour that indicates they could benefit from the service provided, or they have already started to look at product pages and reviews for example.

These types of mailing are extremely valuable and some of the highest engagement emails you can send as they are directly triggered and sent automatically based on a customer action and behaviour. Because they are automated, it also means you can set them up and they'll run 24/7, generating constant revenue for your business.

eF⦿CUS
Marketing

CLIENT CASE STUDY

Client Type: Retail

Objective: Create an optimised strategy for a structured abandoned basket email series to recover potentially lost customers and increase revenue.

Situation

This client was looking for quick-win ways to increase revenue as well as better help their potential customers through to making a purchase. Of those customers who added items into their online basket, many were simply leaving without making a purchase, but there was no campaign currently set up to target these customers with any kind of follow-up, leaving revenue on the table.

Challenges

With a limited amount of resources available internally to devise and implement new campaigns, this client needed assistance to plan, design and set up their new campaign, as well as to devise an ongoing testing strategy to ensure results were maximised.

The main challenge was to ensure the content of the emails stood out from other abandoned basket emails the customer may receive, by using personalisation and ensuring common reasons for this behaviour where addresses. The timing of the emails being sent was also tested to ensure optimal results were achieved at each step.

Solution

eFocus Marketing conducted an in-depth consultancy project to devise a strategy to implement and optimise a new abandoned basket campaign. An initial series was implemented, which initially consisted of two emails sent at 24 and 48 hours after the basket had been abandoned.

In stage two of the implementation, an additional email was added two hours after the basket had been abandoned (once additional data work to make this possible had taken place). There was increased personalisation as other related products that might be of interest, based on the items in the basket, were also suggested in email two and three.

We also made sure that regular customers and/or those who had purchased recently were excluded from any emails sent within the first few hours of the basket being abandoned, and then added into the series later on if they had not naturally gone on to convert.

This campaign saw click rates upwards of 6% and click-to-open rates upwards of 35%, as well as £250,000+ in additional revenue in the first six months after implementation.

3. Purchase and Experience Stage

When someone has made the decision to make a purchase, it is your job to nurture them through the process.

This is an area of customer service that many companies are extremely lacking in because they don't see it as a revenue-generating campaign. However, in both the short and long term, ensuring that customers are well looked after during this stage can have massive benefits.

By putting your customer and the experience they have with your business at the forefront of your messaging, you create trust and loyalty, which in turn can lead to repeat purchases.

Consider the messaging you send post-purchase – do you currently send just the standard messaging? An order confirmation, order despatched and perhaps even a review request email? Or, do you go above and beyond to really make sure that the customer's purchase experience is completely supported by your email marketing? If not, creating a product and brand education series is a great way to do this.

Consider this: a customer buys a beauty product from you – why not send them an email with a short video showing them how to use the product properly? If a customer buys a shed from you, send them instructions on how to construct it properly and ensure the roof felt is properly attached so that it doesn't leak.

By analysing the information available within your organisation, such as the main reasons why customers return items or call customer service post-purchase, you can use this stage to send emails that address these concerns up front and not only have the chance to reduce returns and deliver a high level of customer service, but also to possibly reduce the number of calls to your customer service team as you are already providing this information they are currently asking them for.

In the case of B2B organisations, this post-purchase period is the perfect chance to on-board the customer and properly set expectations about how the relationship will proceed throughout the project/service being delivered. If you are providing a system, for example, use these emails to showcase key elements of the system or how to make the most of its features and how to seek help.

In the short term, these post-purchase emails can also be used to upsell and cross-sell other items to complement and accompany their last purchase – immediately generating the opportunity for increased revenue.

4. Loyalty and Repeat Purchase Stage
Once the purchase has been made and the item delivered, it's time to make your customers feel special and encourage a repeat purchase.

Many of the campaigns you send in this stage will be the same as in the Research and Consideration stage: informational newsletters, regular sales (including promotional) campaigns, and back-in-stock messages etc.

But in this stage, you also want to go one step further. Consider the following:

- How can you encourage loyalty to your brand? Can you treat customers differently from non-customers? Can you segment your best, most loyal customers and treat them differently from those who have only purchased once or twice?

- How can you encourage current customers to recommend you to others? Think about a refer-a-friend campaign, or asking them to share their purchases and experience with your brand on social media, for example.

- How can you make your customers feel special? Perhaps offer them a discount/free offer on their birthday, or celebrate the anniversary of their first purchase with your brand, for example.

- A replenishment series – do you have a product that needs renewing at specific intervals? For example, beauty products that you know last for three months if used daily? Consider sending a series of emails in the run-up to/just after this time to encourage a repeat purchase.

5. Reactivation Stage

Email marketing reactivation strategies help to clean up your database, reduce wasted emails and bring back potentially important customers, which can lead to increased conversion rates and revenue.

There are two main areas to focus in on in terms of reactivating your subscribers.

1. Re-Engage Inactive Subscribers

Although there will be a number of subscribers who are no longer interested in receiving your content and who will not be able to be re-engaged, it is crucial to establish those who are no longer opening or clicking on your emails and can be reactivated as opposed to those who may eventually need to be removed from your list. This will allow you to get a true picture of the value of your subscriber list and the health of your database.

Although some subscribers may unsubscribe or register a complaint, many will just fall inactive.

Studies have shown that as many as 60% of the subscribers on a typical list will not have opened or clicked on an email in the past six months.

With the cost of acquiring new subscribers significantly higher than that of re-engaging those who have lapsed, strategies to reconnect with these subscribers can generate an attractive ROI.

The aim of this strategy is to solicit a response – either for the subscriber to open or click on an email or to unsubscribe.

These 'reactivation campaigns' involve starting to send a series of emails to subscribers who are starting to show signs of inactivity (passive subscribers), through to the point at which you deem them to have not opened or clicked on an email in so long that they are inactive with your programme.

Throughout this series you would differentiate your messages from your normal strategy and even give exclusive special offers in order to elicit a response.

If, after these communications, they still don't engage with your email marketing, you may want to then consider going one step further and implementing a 're-permissioning campaign'.

This involves seeking a subscriber's consent to continue to send them marketing messages. If they do not respond and positively indicate that they would like to continue to receive mailings, you would then remove them from your list.

There are a couple of schools of thought around this.

i. The first is that if you are seeing deliverability issues, this situation can be helped by removing inactive subscribers – one area that mailbox providers consider is the engagement subscribers have with your mailings. If you have a large portion of your database who are inactive and not opening your emails, this could have a negative impact on your delivery rates.

ii. The second is that you should also look at this strategy with data from the wider business before re-permission and removing subscribers from your list. This would include looking at purchase data to make this decision; just landing in the inbox, even if they don't open the email, could be prompting them subconsciously to make a purchase – especially for retailers with physical stores.

When looking at email activity, defining an inactive subscriber is very much dependent on the frequency of emails you send. For example, if you only send once a month, the opportunity to interact is very much lower than a company sending daily. Therefore, the time frame within which you would define activity is different in each case.

Taking a basic example of a company sending once or twice a week, you may choose to define an inactive subscriber as anyone who has not opened or clicked on an email in the last 12 months.

However, you may decide to further segment email engagement and define stages leading up to this point in order to target them with messaging differently depending on their level of activity. For example:

Active – opened or clicked on an email in the last 3 months
Passive – opened or clicked on an email in the last 6 months
Inactive – not opened or clicked on an email in the last 9 months +

It may also be prudent to identify customers who are active in different ways with your programme – for example, the needs of someone who is opening your emails but not clicking, vs. someone not interacting at all, are very different.

Non-openers are much less engaged – looking at your subject lines is the first place to start testing changes to encourage increased engagement.

Non-clickers are at least opening the messages they are receiving. With these subscribers you need to figure out why they are opening and then not clicking. For example, is it that they are interested in the subject line but then aren't interested in the products shown? This may indicate a disconnect between your subject lines and your content, including the 'wrong' sort of information in your emails, or even that your design needs to be further optimised to better encourage conversion.

2. Encourage Inactive Customers to Buy Again

It is also prudent to create a campaign to target customers who are no longer buying from you (haven't made another purchase within a specified amount of time – remember, this will differ depending on your business and average purchase frequency that you would expect).

I would recommend implementing this type of campaign at various stages as the customer becomes more inactive. For example, if your normal buying cycle is once a month and a customer hasn't purchased again after three months, send a reminder email. Then after six months and nine months send two further reminders. If after 12 months they still haven't come back, consider sending a special offer to reactivate them.

Ensure that the content in these emails is personalised to their previous behaviour and, if possible, reference their last purchase to remind them of the interaction they had with you. Depending on whether the customer has previously purchased from you once or multiple times, this should also alter the type and tone of the content and offers you send during this campaign.

You could also layer your segmentation here to identify both types of inactivity and again target your messaging accordingly:

a) Inactive customers who are currently active with your email programme.
b) Inactive customers who are currently passive with your email programme.
c) Inactive customers who are currently inactive with your email programme.

✎ TAKE ACTION

- Conduct a customer journey workshop

  o Gather together members of your business from different teams (including different areas of marketing and customer service for example).

  o Think about each stage of the customer journey:
     1. Sign-up/acquisition and discovery
     2. Research and consideration
     3. Purchase and experience
     4. Loyalty and repeat purchase
     5. Reactivation

  Ask yourself the following five questions:

     1. What tasks are they completing?
     2. What touchpoints are they interacting with to achieve these tasks?
     3. What are they trying to achieve?
     4. How do they feel at this stage in their journey?
     5. What questions are they looking to get answered?

  See Appendix 7 on page 308 for an example.

  Also think about the content you already have/need to create to meet the needs you have identified above.

- Prioritise possible new campaigns based on impact and ease of implementation

  Once you've conducted an exercise with your team to map your customer journey, and you've done the audit of all the current campaigns running in your business, the next step is to evaluate the new campaigns you want to add into your strategy as we discussed at the beginning of this chapter.

Identify the new campaigns you could implement at each stage – which will make the biggest difference to your subscribers?

Campaign description	Ease of implementation (1-10 – 10 being easiest to implement)	Potential impact (1-10 – 10 being highest impact)	Total score

By doing this quick analysis, you'll be able to focus your effort and resources on those that will have the biggest impact/be the easiest to implement in your business first, propelling you forward.

With many of my clients, if no automations are currently in place at the moment, the top three that I focus on to start with to quickly drive revenue include:

1. abandoned basket email
2. abandoned browse email (product/category level)
3. repeat purchase campaign (follow-up from sale)

If you already have these in place in your business, optimise them – implement a document testing strategy, add to the campaign series and improve what you're already doing – before moving on to implement further campaigns.

You can download a copy of this as a worksheet here: www.etelligencebook.com/members/step3/customerjourney/

• If applicable, create your lead scoring strategy including identifying different activities and their level of interest.

3.3

Multichannel Marketing

Multichannel marketing is the implementation of a single strategy across multiple channels, maximising opportunities to interact with and engage prospective customers.

This comprises of both offline and online channels including email, print, TV and radio ads, your website, promotional events, mobile apps, SMS messaging, a product's packaging, catalogues, retail locations and word-of-mouth.

The goal is to allow prospects to buy your products/services through the channel of their choice. Multichannel marketing once again puts the customer at the forefront of everything you are doing – making sure that you are where your customers are.

Research suggests that multichannel customers spend three to four times more than single-channel customers do.

The best multichannel campaigns provide a seamless experience, so that no matter what channel a customer chooses to interact with your business, the response (in all ways: speed, tone of voice and outcome) should be consistent.

You need to consider how you can best use your marketing channels at different stages of the customer journey for different purposes, but with that cohesive message and purpose.

For example, creating campaigns that utilise multiple channels together:

- Consider adding in SMS messaging as part of your communication series to drive people back to re-engage with your email content (this could work well if the subscriber has not interacted with any emails in the series).

- Add a targeted piece of direct mail or use retargeting campaigns (using custom lists) on social media (for example, Facebook) or search (for example, Google) to reinforce welcome and on-boarding email series messaging.

How and when you utilise each channel will also depend on your objectives. Email marketing and social media, for example, serve very different purposes in your overall marketing strategy – email is generally more adept at driving focused traffic and direct conversions, while social media is better for engaging directly with your audience in conversations and for sharing.

There are various challenges to implementing a multichannel marketing strategy, including:

- **having multiple touchpoints leads to more complexity**
  Creating a multichannel strategy means having a cohesive message across a number of channels, and a continuous evolution of that message as more data is gathered on each customer. It is important to constantly develop and coordinate campaigns that span multiple channels in a way that the customer finds meaningful and trustworthy.

- **additional time and resources may be needed to build a successful multichannel marketing strategy**
  Not only will resources be required to plan and implement these types of campaigns, but also, as more data is collected, this will also lead to a need for new tools or data platforms, and staff to be able to understand the data.

- **multi-team participation required**

  In many businesses, these different channels are run by different teams with different agendas, objectives and priorities. It's therefore entirely possible for a customer to move across every channel and have a vastly different experience within each one.

  Different departments within the business need to be constantly aligned in their objectives and strategy, as well as the data being utilised. This once again brings us back to the need for a single customer view with the ability to track customers' communications they receive across every channel to ensure that each are targeting the same prospect in a meaningful and cohesive way.

- **difficulties with attribution**

  Without the right attribution model being chosen and successfully implemented, there is often confusion as to which channel was responsible for generating a conversion: actually, it's often a combination of channels that led to it.

  However, without the correct attribution model in place, it can be hard for you to make informed decisions on budgeting and resources – knowing what triggered each response enables you to assess whether or not your marketing efforts are getting the best results.

These challenges need to be overcome in order to implement a successful multichannel marketing strategy within your business.

E-telligence: Email marketing isn't dead, the way you're using it is

CHAPTER 4

GROW
Your Audience

Imagine this...

You spend time, money and effort driving traffic to your website. But the majority of people who visit are likely not ready to make a purchase yet. Without gaining an opt-in, these prospects will simply leave your website and possibly never return.

Users will stay on a web page for only a few seconds unless something catches their attention. If you can offer a really enticing opt-in and encourage these visitors to subscribe to receive your emails, you then have the ability to continue to contact them on an ongoing basis, and nurture them to make a purchase.

Having a prominent email opt-in on your website is a great way to capture information from those visitors that are ready to buy from you, but also (and most importantly) from those that would otherwise have left your website without purchasing anything.

In this chapter we will cover the three tasks we have already looked at in this book for the rest of your email marketing activity, but this time, related specifically to your list growth:

1. Auditing your existing activities
2. Optimising what you currently have in place
3. Filling the gaps in your list growth strategy

Quantifying Your Email List

The first place to start evaluating your email programme is to quantify your current efforts.

The three main statistics to calculate and keep track of are:

1. Your Email List Growth Rate

You should monitor email list growth to ensure subscriber numbers are increasing and not in a gradual decline.

Your email list growth rate is the rate at which the database is growing – considering those who are joining and those who are leaving within a chosen time frame (for example, 12 months).

It can be calculated using the following formula:

$$\frac{(\text{Number of new subscribers}) \text{ minus } (\text{Number of unsubscribes} + \text{bounces} + \text{spam complaints})}{\text{Total no. of email addresses on your list (today)}} \times 100$$

2. Your Email Subscriber Lifetime Value

Your email subscriber lifetime value is a calculation of the projected revenue that an email subscriber will generate during their lifetime.

This helps you to work out how much you can afford to spend to acquire a new subscriber and how much revenue this will ultimately provide in return. In this calculation, rather than taking the lifetime value of a customer to your business overall, we are specifically looking at it through an email marketing lens and the lifetime of the email subscription.

In order to calculate this value at a basic level, use the following data for the last 12 months:

- **Total email profits** (revenue minus costs – effectively your ROI)

- **Total number of active email addresses on your list** (those who have not bounced/unsubscribed and are active with your email programme – i.e. have opened an email within a specific time frame, for example, six months)

- **Average lifetime of an email subscriber** (the time between when they subscribe and when they become inactive with your email programme)

Put this data into the following formula:

$$\frac{\text{Total email marketing profit}}{\text{Total no. of active email addresses}}$$

This will give you the amount of profit each active subscriber will generate in a year.

THEN

Multiply this number by the average lifetime of an email subscriber to get your overall email subscriber lifetime value.

You could also work this out on an individual subscriber basis to help identify those who are most valuable to your business and treat them slightly differently from those with lower values.

3. Your Attrition Rate

Growing your email list is a marathon not a sprint; it's important to continually focus on adding new people onto your email list for two main reasons:

- Grow further and communicate with more prospects and customers

- Replace those that leave – this is called your Attrition Rate (or Churn Rate) and for email marketing will be made up of:

  1. unsubscribes

  2. bounces (hard and soft bounces) – these are removed from your database dependent on your ESP's rules (we recommend that hard bounces are removed immediately and soft bounces after three to five consecutive instances – although this will differ depending on your send strategy and frequency)

  3. spam complaints (these should be removed immediately after notification through your feedback loop – see Chapter 5 for more information about your complaint rate).

Attrition can account for a loss of about 25-30% of the average email list every year.

Your list growth efforts have to outpace your list's attrition rate; otherwise, no matter how much list-building you do, your email list will stay the same size or even shrink.

As also discussed in more detail in Chapter 5, email lists must be cleaned and maintained to ensure that messages reach the inbox. Spam complaints and bounces have an impact on email deliverability, as mailbox providers (for example, Microsoft, Gmail, Oath etc.) set thresholds for these statistics, particularly spam complaints.

If your email marketing is consistently being sent to invalid or unwanted email addresses, you could find your messages filtered as spam, your account blocked, or at worst, suspended from sending mail altogether from your IP or domain.

There are multiple ways to calculate your attrition rate, but the way I do it for my clients is to pick a time frame (usually the last 12 months), add up the subscribers you've lost during this time (unsubscribes, bounces and complaints), and then divide this number by the size of your list on the day you're calculating your attrition rate (don't use the count of your list size from a year ago).

$$\frac{\text{Unsubscribes + hard and soft bounces + spam complaints}}{\text{List size (today)}}$$

Setting Targets for Your List Growth

Setting targets specifically for your list growth allows you to know where you are going, create a targeted plan to get there, see how you are measuring up along the way and adjust and refine what you are doing in order to meet these targets.

It allows you to know that you are continuously moving forward with your strategy and growing your email list with <u>the right kind</u> of subscribers – those who are your target audience. Revisit your customer persona work – WHO exactly is it that you want to target, WHERE are you most likely to find them on/offline and HOW can you best attract them onto your email list? What do they need from you in order to say *'YES, I want to receive emails from you and find out more about your products/services'*?

Focus on quality over quantity.

If you target your advertising and therefore list-building efforts accordingly, you will ensure that your email list is full of those who are more likely to engage with your emails and ultimately to buy from you.

When setting your targets, consider:

- What is your list growth budget?

- Looking at your Email Subscriber Lifetime Value, how much can you afford to spend to acquire each new subscriber (cost per acquisition – CPA)?

Using these two numbers, you can work out how many subscribers you estimate being able to generate.

You should also look at your attrition rate – does the number you just calculated allow you to grow your email list past those you are losing each year? If not, you need to reconsider your list growth budget and CPA.

 TAKE ACTION

- Gather the following data about your list growth:

  o What is the current size of your email list?

  o Collect the following data for the last 12 months:
    - total email marketing revenue
    - total email profits (revenue minus costs – effectively your ROI)
    - total number of active email addresses on your list (those who have not bounced/unsubscribed and are active with your email programme – i.e. have opened an email within a specific time frame)
    - average lifetime of an email subscriber – the time between when they subscribe and when they become inactive
    - number of new subscribers
    - unsubscribes
    - bounces (hard and soft bounces)
    - spam complaints

- Using these figures, calculate your list growth metrics:

  o Email list growth rate

  o Average email subscriber lifetime value

  o Attrition rate

You can download a copy of this as a worksheet here:
www.etelligencebook.com/members/step4/quantify/

4.2

Your Current Sign-Up Process

Once you know how many people are joining your email list, you should also evaluate the way in which these opt-ins are being generated.

The next step in your audit is to review your current sign-up process including:

- your data collection sources
- opt-in type
- sign-up form format and placement

Your Data Collection Sources

How you acquire new addresses onto your list will have a big impact on the performance of your programme going forward.

Different types of data will have a different way of interacting with your campaigns, different needs and ultimately a different lifetime value for your business. By different types of data, I mean those with different levels of buying intent at the time of signing up, and those who have landed on your website from different traffic sources. It's important to know where your data is coming from and which sources of sign-ups are most productive and valuable for your business in both the short and long term – this is where you should focus your attention for this part of the audit.

Traffic-driving activities you are currently engaged in may include:

- organic social media posts
- paid ads (social media channel ads – for example, Facebook, search engine Pay per Click (PPC) ads, etc.)
- print advertising
- affiliate marketing
- TV advertising
- radio advertising
- partnerships
- in-store advertising

Think about how you are currently driving traffic to your website and individual landing pages or squeeze pages encouraging an email opt-in, and analyse which are the best and worst performing in terms of conversion rate to sign-up.

A squeeze page is a page dedicated to one purpose – in this case gaining an opt-in. It has no distractions and no other actions that can be taken from the page other than to sign up. These types of pages are best used when driving traffic from paid ads to maximise conversion rate and value gained from the activity.

A landing page on the other hand is in the normal style of your site, including your header and links to other areas of the site that the user can navigate to, away from that page.

By tracking which data sources are generating the sign-ups you are seeing, you can evaluate where best to spend your marketing budget – if one data source is spending a lot of money but not driving good quality sign-ups (subscribers that are not engaging or buying from you once on your list) or has a low conversion rate to opt-in, consider moving your marketing budget to those that perform better in these areas.

Different Types of Opt-In

When growing your email list, it is important to gain a clear and positive opt-in. This involves a prospect giving absolute permission for you to maintain contact with them (in this case via email) – it is a positive action to say *'Yes! I want to receive emails from you'*.

Gaining an opt-in is a legal requirement for marketing communications in many countries. It is usually achieved through a tick box (as part of an account sign-up or purchase process, for example) or a standalone form dedicated to one purpose: getting the opt-in.

If using a checkbox to meet this need, ensure that it is unchecked when first seen by the customer, so that a positive and definite action takes place when the box is clicked, and they agree to receive communications from you.

Single Opt-In

A single opt-in involves getting permission in just one step, allowing you to immediately communicate with the subscriber via email after the completion of the form. This means that anyone filling in your form and clicking 'Submit' will be added to your database.

A certain percentage of your new subscribers may provide 'fake' email addresses (either an address that doesn't exist at all or a secondary email address that they rarely check) and some may accidentally enter the wrong email, for example, leaving off a letter or spelling part of it incorrectly.

One way to combat some of these issues is to use a third-party tool such as BriteVerify or FreshAddress which will check and verify the email address being entered to stop invalid addresses being added to your list.

Double Opt-In

Double opt-in involves a subscriber completing your sign-up form and then immediately being sent an email which asks them to click to confirm they really do want to subscribe.

When it comes to the content of the double opt-in email, it has a very distinct purpose – to get the user to click to confirm their subscription. This email should not be confused with the welcome email – these two messages have very different purposes and should be kept separate.

Double opt-in is the best of the best in terms of opt-in processes – it checks an email address is real and validates that that person definitely wants to receive those emails, as well as getting an action immediately from the subscriber.

Double opt-in therefore can be a very valuable process to gaining slightly more engaged subscribers, help keep an accidental pristine spam trap from being added to your list, or an unintended recipient, who may then be more likely to mark your email as spam, all of which can damage your sender reputation and affect deliverability.

However, despite these benefits, a simple fact remains – you are adding an additional step to the sign-up process which can result in a slightly lower number of sign-ups. The more barriers you put in place of someone before they can complete an action, the more people will drop off along the way and not reach your end goal for them – in this case, to confirm their email address and be added to your list.

If you want to increase conversions, you need to remove all the obstacles you can and make each remaining step as simple, frictionless and fast as possible; double opt-in of course goes against this.

Additionally, if a subscriber doesn't receive the double opt-in email (due to the wrong email address being entered or deliverability problems for example), they will not have the chance to confirm their address – however much they may want to!

Many marketers accept a drop off of around the 20–40% mark in sign-ups by using double opt-in (although not much data exists from specific studies). And because of this, your list will not grow as quickly as it would if you were using a single opt-in method.

Do You Have to Use Double Opt-in to Get Good Engagement Rates from Your List?

NO! Although some people do find their double opt-in list to be highly responsive, there is no reason why a single opt-in list can't be just as responsive if managed well. You need to use the type of opt-in most suitable for the situation your business is in.

For example, if you have good data sources (organically collected sign-ups from targeted, good quality traffic sources) and are at a minimal risk from low quality data, you won't necessarily need or want to use double opt-in. For example, direct sign-ups coming in from your own website.

But it can prove handy when using data sources where you are unsure of data quality such as affiliate or co-registration websites or when addresses are being collected in-store or at a call centre where they may be input incorrectly.

In some countries, such as Germany and Canada, double opt-in is often used as a way to deliver definitive proof of sign-up to meet legal requirements; the level of confirmation required by the laws in these countries makes double opt-in a robust way of actually meeting the requirements (although the process itself is not explicitly required by law at this time).

Double opt-in can also be useful to implement if you've experienced deliverability issues in the past due to data quality. However, I would suggest that if this is the case, using double opt-in would just be the tip of the iceberg and much more investigation should be taking place into the source of data, for example.

If you are using double opt-in, here are some ways to maximise conversion:

- Optimise the landing page after sign-up – customise it and warn subscribers of the next step they need to take and what happens if they don't. Use the FOMO (Fear of Missing Out) principle to let them know that without clicking on the link to confirm, they will not be subscribed and will not receive all the wonderful things you promised them straight to their email account.

  Prompt them to check their spam/junk folder (or Gmail promotional tab) in case the email is delivered there, and you can even give them the option on this page to resend the double opt-in email if they have not received it within a certain amount of time.

- Make the subject line of your double opt-in email very clear – this is an important email that they need to act on to confirm their subscription, so the first step is to get them to open it.

- Don't mix other content in with this email – keep it clear and to the point with just one action to take – to confirm the subscription.

- Resend the double opt-in email after 24/48 hours if a subscriber hasn't confirmed – you could even consider sending a third attempt after this in case the subscriber hasn't received the message through deliverability issues for example.

- And don't forget about the confirmation page after the subscriber has clicked – don't just leave them hanging! Direct them to useful areas of your website or specific products or categories of product to keep up the action momentum!

Regardless of your opt-in type...

As a marketer or business owner, you should be concerned with the quality of the data you are driving to your opt-in, as well as the quality of your strategy and how you engage subscribers going forward. After all, a sign-up alone doesn't generate revenue; you need to provide valuable, relevant and interesting content on an ongoing basis too.

Sign-Up Form Format and Placement

The way in which you present your opt-in is critical to maximising your conversion rates to opt in.

The placement of the form on your website, the wording you use and the additional opt-in offers that you offer can all have an impact. As part of this audit process, you should look at every instance in which potential customers have the opportunity to sign up to your email list, both on and offline and evaluate the effectiveness of each instance.

In the next section we'll talk more about optimising your sign-up form to maximise conversions.

CASE STUDY

Client Type: Roadside assistance

Objective: Remove invalid, duplicate, and deliverable but problematic addresses from their list.

Situation

AAA Ohio uses email marketing to communicate with its 760,000 members in the state. In 1999 the company launched a simple email newsletter that today has grown to include news, features, and special offers. In 2016, the club sent 17 million email messages to nearly 600,000 recipients, using a mix of targeted and broadcast messaging. The decision to invest in email address quality was an easy one for AAA Ohio, because the club knows how valuable the right email addresses are to revenue, renewals, and member contact.

Challenges

AAA Ohio had been building its email list since 1999 without focusing on list hygiene. The organisation had been pulling data from a variety of legacy systems to build out its database. As a result, AAA Ohio suspected that they had a high number of invalid, duplicate, and deliverable but problematic addresses, which required removal. This presented a major problem for the organisation because it knows that members for whom it has a working email address spend $75 more per year on average. This fact, coupled with recent news of a competitor that found itself on a blacklist, was the driving force behind AAA Ohio's decision to hire a trusted vendor to help it maintain a clean email list.

The Solution

AAA Ohio leveraged the full service SafeToSend solution to flag 31.5% of its database as invalid or problematic and identify 2,200 toxic spam trap addresses for suppression.

After completing the hygiene process, the client experienced a multitude of benefits, including:

- decrease in undeliverable email addresses from 25% to 6.5%
- a boost in email deliverability from 97% to nearly 100%
- a 20% lift in email engagement
- an estimated $59,175 in additional value provided by 789 suggested FreshAddress corrections.

4.3
Optimising Your Sign-Up Form to Maximise Conversions

To maximise your chances of converting a browser into a subscriber, make sure these six key areas of your sign-up form are optimised:

1. **Have a strong headline**

   Make your headlines succinct, specific, and compelling, following up with copy delivering more information to entice the prospect to act.

   Your objective here is to create a compelling headline that is either benefit-driven (by this I mean it focuses on the benefits the subscriber will receive) or hits on a specific problem or wish that the subscribers you would like to attract have. It should be kept short and sweet whilst grabbing the attention of the user.

2. **Be clear in your copy**

   The copy used on your sign-up form has a direct and measurable effect on conversion rates; therefore, it is important to spend time crafting and testing the wording. People want to know what they're signing up for and why they should give you their details.

   A strong form grabs the subscriber's attention and gives prospects a good reason to say: 'Yes, sign me up!'

   Set subscriber expectations in terms of what you will send, when you will send it and the benefits to them of receiving, opening, and reading your emails. For example: 'Register now and get our latest offers, exclusive email-only discounts, and the latest trends sent straight to your inbox twice a week!'

Be direct and focus on what will capture their interest. Succinctly convey the key elements of what they will receive from you and clearly highlight the value to the subscriber.

The rule of three is a great technique to follow here. This is a writing principle based on the premise that people tend to remember three things better than two, four or more. Having three things makes it easy to remember and combines both brevity and rhythm with having the smallest amount of information to create a pattern. This tactic has been employed famously throughout history:

- *Stop, Look and Listen* – public safety message
- *The Good, the Bad and the Ugly* – film title
- *'Veni, vidi, vici'* (I came, I saw, I conquered) – Julius Caesar
- *Liberté, égalité, fraternité* – the slogan of the French Republic predating 1790
- *A Mars a day helps you work, rest and play* – Mars advertising slogan since 1959

So, the main thing to consider here is, what are the three main things I want my potential customers to know and remember?

3. Be open, honest and transparent

This form is often the first impression of your business for many users. So it's really important to start the relationship off in the right way and tell people exactly what they will receive and when, so that there are no nasty surprises when they start to receive your emails!

By setting their expectations properly at the point of sign-up, you will ensure that the people who register really want to receive your communications and are interested in what you offer. This will also help to ensure a low complaint rate (subscribers pressing the spam/junk button) and higher positive engagement (opens, clicks, conversions etc.) with your campaigns going forward.

4. Make the form easy to use

Ensure your sign-up forms are not overly complicated, as well as simple to read and understand. If you can, use systems that make the sign-up form more intuitive (such as completing common email addresses and postal addresses from just postcodes etc.); this will also help people to complete the form quickly and easily.

- Consider how you display your sign-up form – if you find a lot of people fail to complete it, consider reducing the number of data fields you ask for. Even though some of your data fields may be optional, at a glance people only perceive the overall number of fields.

- To encourage users to subscribe and gather slightly more information, consider using a two-step (or chained page) approach to increase subscriber conversion; this involves the subscriber completing a series of short forms. If they navigate away, the data is still captured up to that point.

- Use cookie technology to recognise when users re-engage with your content, and, rather than repeating the same information again, request additional information from them; use pre-populated information where possible, making it as easy as possible for them to engage.

5. Consider the data fields you collect

It is important to strike a balance on your sign-up form between asking too many questions (which will help you understand your customer well, but may put off subscribers), and too few questions (which will increase the size of your email list, but not allow you to qualify interest and determine characteristics).

Aim to collect, at a minimum, the subscriber's email address and their name (first name or title and surname), so as to help to personalise and target your emails immediately and build trust.

Depending on your business needs, you may decide that other information is critical to also collect during the sign-up process (or afterwards using progressive profiling, such as a survey, poll or behaviour). This is where you need to balance the number of data fields you are asking for, ensuring you maximise conversions to opt in.

Only collect the information you need and are going to use.

The more information you ask for, the less likely they are to complete the form and sign up.

Collect only the information that you NEED on sign-up – so an email address would of course be the minimum level of information needed to register them. However, by asking for items such as first name or what their interests are, you can ensure that you start to personalise your messages from the start of the relationship. So collecting this level of data is highly beneficial.

On the flip side, the more fields you require to be completed (although likely to reduce the number of sign-ups you achieve), those that do opt in will be even more qualified and interested in what you are offering.

So, consider carefully your objectives: these dictate how you will personalise your communications to ensure relevancy and drive the subscriber towards your desired action. You need to decide what fields to collect on sign-up and which could be collected later on in the relationship (such as during the on-boarding process).

6. Create a benefit-driven call-to-action button

The text on your button is critical to encouraging the sign-up.

Standard wording such as 'Sign up', 'Submit', or 'Register' doesn't tell the user what will happen next. For the best results, it is important to be specific and, once again, benefit-driven.

Focus on what the subscriber will gain by submitting the form, for example: 'Get involved', 'Join us', 'Get 10% off your first purchase now', 'Subscribe me to the blog', 'Sign up today for access to free webinars and events' etc.

An opt-in shown as part of a purchase or account sign-up process needs to be considered and tested in terms of its placement within this process, as well as how it is presented in order to ensure it doesn't negatively impact the main reason for the form – to complete the purchase.

For example, consider whether having a non-checked tick box next to the email field or at the end of the form right before the final purchase button would be a better option; test which sees the highest conversion rate to opt in and has the least negative impact on the flow of making a purchase. Also consider the wording used here to encourage a positive action as this can have an enormous impact on conversion rate.

4.4

Making Your Opt-In Attractive

To make a sign-up form extra appealing, many businesses use an additional incentive to secure the opt-in, commonly referred to as an 'opt-in offer' or 'lead magnet' (or even an ethical bribe in some circles!).

An email address is a valuable asset and you need to give people a good reason to give it to you. When they do, you in turn need to engage reciprocity: that is, create a 'value exchange' that provides something of value to your prospect in exchange for use of their data.

The most common and effective opt-in offers for retailers include free postage, a discount off the subscriber's first order, or a free sample offer.

B2B Examples	B2C Examples
A whitepaper or report	A special offer – this could be a percentage discount, or a '£x off' etc.
A checklist/cheat sheet	Giving a free gift with every purchase
Access to a VIP or privilege area within a website	Offering free delivery
Entry to a competition	Providing a free sample

The exact cost of any offer given must be balanced against the lifetime value of the prospective subscriber.

This may mean that not every individual is of equal value to your business; hence you will need to tailor your incentive accordingly.

Furthermore, the incentive will be more effective when directly relevant to the product/service on offer. It is possible that your service is reason enough in itself, but most businesses find that an incentive increases the number of sign-ups.

If you have an incentive in place already, look at your results and consider whether it is the most relevant and enticing offer that could be given to potential subscribers. If not, what else could you test to see if you can increase your conversion rate?

If you don't have an opt-in incentive in place right now, why not test and see if adding one increases your conversion rate and drives, not just an increase in sign-ups, but also in sales, particularly for retailers offering first purchase discounts!

4.5

Post-Sign-Up Strategy

Once a user has submitted the sign-up form, you should take them to a dedicated page (or pop-up window for example) to thank them and confirm the sign-up.

On this page, also consider adding:

- **a note to look out for your first email** – for example, a double opt-in or welcome email in their inbox. If you are using a double opt-in, remind the subscriber to act on this email (giving them the subject line makes it easier for them to spot in their inbox).

- **a whitelisting prompt** – this asks the subscriber to add your sending domain to their address book, allowing you to bypass some of the spam filters set and land in their inbox. Consider providing a link to a page on your site that gives them further instructions of how to do this in the most common email clients – for example Microsoft (Hotmail), Gmail and Oath (Yahoo!) etc.

- **social media sharing and follow links** – whilst you have the user in the flow of connecting with you, direct them to like or follow you on your social media channels, and/or encourage them to share the sign-up with their friends.

- **direction to other relevant places on your website** – where do you want subscribers to go next? What should they look at or be aware of on your website? Think about how you can keep them moving through a journey with you.

  For example, on a B2B site, subscribers could be directed to blogs or relevant service information pages. On a B2C site, being directed to popular categories of product or bestselling/currently trending products would be more appropriate.

And of course, as we have already discussed, the next step in the customer journey is to implement a welcome and on-boarding email series to nurture the new subscriber and encourage their first purchase.

4.6

Advertise Your Opt-In

You should look to promote your sign-up anywhere a touchpoint with prospects exists.

The first question to ask is: 'Where are the people I want to attract hanging out?' In online terms, this means looking at your web traffic (i.e. to see where people visiting your website are coming from). This information can also be gleaned from your customer persona work.

Once you know where the people you want to attract are, you can then target them with opportunities to interact with your brand, including signing up to your email programme.

6 Ways to Build Your Email List

1. Through your website

To optimise every opportunity to convert the traffic you're most likely already driving to your website into email subscribers, ensure your sign-up form is placed in strategic and effective places on your site.

For example:

- **On your homepage** – include a sign-up call-to-action or form in the top half of the homepage, so that it can be seen without the user having to scroll down (perhaps using a feature box). Remember that the homepage is the first page many new website visitors land on. If their attention is not grabbed quickly, they may leave and not come back.

- **In the header menu** – including a call-to-action to sign up in your header menu is effective because this is where browsers are looking when exploring your site. Any links provided here will be directed to the relevant landing page (which will include your sign-up form and more information).

- **In a pod within the footer area** – adding a sign-up pod to your website footer allows subscribers to enter their details from wherever they are on the site. It is a quick way to capture their data and a place where many people will expect to find a sign-up option.

- **In your sidebar** – if you have a sidebar, add a sign-up form as it will be visible on many pages throughout your website. Note that the optimal placement is at the top of your sidebar.

- **In the middle and at the bottom of blog posts** – if someone reads to the end of one of your blog posts, they most likely have been intrigued by or liked what they were reading. This is a perfect opportunity to offer them more by providing a sign-up box at the end of the post.

- **During the account sign-up and purchase process** – when someone is registering for an account or making a purchase, ensure you add a non-checked opt-in box to allow them to subscribe to receive marketing communications from you.

- **In pop-ups** – pop-ups are the Marmite of the marketing world; you either love them or you hate them. But using a well-timed and designed pop-up can be a great way to increase your conversions to sign-up.

The beauty of pop-ups is their intrusive nature but just be careful not to annoy site visitors and be mindful of how they display on mobile devices (note that Google will now penalise you for a badly displayed pop-up on a mobile device).

o Consider your pop-up timing

Just because someone is interacting with you online doesn't mean it's right to pounce on them straight away!

Think about this situation in real life... you walk into a shop and a sales person immediately accosts you, asking if you'd like to sign up to receive offers. You may have never been in the shop before, you don't know what they offer, or if you even like or need the products or services they provide. It's most likely intimidating, pushy, irritating and not the right time to make an offer. The same is true of pop-ups and why some people don't like them!

Instead of immediately triggering a pop-up as soon as someone reaches your site, consider using one of the following types:

— *Time-delayed pop-up* – enables the user to read some content first before seeing your pop-up, therefore helping them to self-qualify whether they are interested in what you offer. The best way to determine how long to delay the pop-up is to check your site analytics (for example, Google Analytics). Have a look at the average bounce time for the page and set the pop-up just before this time. Don't forget, this is likely shorter or longer for different pages on your site.

— *After-scroll pop-up* – again, this delays the time until the pop-up is shown, but in this case, it's based on the user action and only shows when they scroll to a certain point on the page.

— *On-click pop-up* – activated by the user clicking on a CTA button to subscribe, for example.

— *On-exit pop-up* – this type of pop-up activates when a user navigates their mouse towards the 'X' to close down the internet window, offering one final opportunity to encourage the sign-up before they leave your site.

There are lots of different types of pop-ups - the key is finding the right fit for your website (and each page on your website) and ensuring that it is well-designed, clearly states the benefits of signing up and is easy to close if the user does not want to complete the form.

You should also consider using cookie tracking so as not to show the pop-up again too often – for example, only show to the same user (who is not already a subscriber) once every 60 days.

Similarly, you wouldn't want to show your 'subscribe now' request to anyone currently on the email list – it's not a great idea to interrupt your existing subscribers with a request for something they are already part of and is a great way to ensure they don't feel valued as well as showing that your brand doesn't care about its customers!

You may also want to offer a different message to someone who was previously on the email list and has since unsubscribed, to encourage re-subscription, and to those who have purchased from you previously but are not currently signed up to receive emails.

o   Evaluate your pop-up placement.

You should also consider what is appropriate for each page – how you want to interact with users coming onto your homepage is likely different from how you would treat those visiting product pages. For example, homepage visitors are likely new visitors who are looking around, may not know what they want yet and need to be treated differently from those visiting specific product pages/categories where their interest is already more defined.

o What will your offer be?

Similarly, the offer you give should differ by page – for example, to reference the category they have visited: 'Looking to update your summer wardrobe? Sign up and receive 10% off your first order!' or 'Looking to update your winter wardrobe? Sign up and receive 10% off your first order!'

As always, testing thoroughly is the best way to ensure you gain the best results from your pop-up placement, offer and timing.

2. Social media (organic/paid ads)

Advertise your email sign-up through your social media channels. Email remains a significantly more effective way to acquire new customers than social media – nearly 40 times that of Facebook and Twitter combined.

Create regular posts to entice your subscribers to sign up including teasers of upcoming email topics or offers, your opt-in incentive (if applicable) and the benefits of receiving your emails. And don't forget it goes both ways... Include social sharing and 'connect' buttons in your emails to drive the conversation through those channels as well.

3. Search Engine Marketing (SEM) (including Pay per Click advertising and natural search)

Driving traffic to your website or squeeze pages to encourage email opt-ins is a targeted way to grow your email list. This can be achieved through:

- PPC – specific, targeted ads to drive traffic to squeeze pages for specific search terms.

- Retargeting – this involves showing ads to people who have already visited certain pages on your website and further encouraging them to take a desired action; in this case, it could be a further incentive to sign up if they haven't already.

- SEO – optimising your website pages to target specific keywords and phrases that your ideal clients are searching for.

4. Content marketing

Using content to entice subscribers and show your authority – either on your own website or on other people's sites, always including a call-to-action back to sign-up to receive more great information or offers from you!

This could include:

- blogs (guest blogs on other sites)
- webinars
- podcasting
- membership area content

5. Print ads

If you're running any type of print ads, whether that be magazine or newspaper ads, leaflets given out at events or those sent within a customer's order package, make sure you are displaying the benefits of being part of your email marketing programme and encouraging the reader to sign up. This could be through a link to visit, a text-to-sign-up programme or even using a QR code that takes them to a sign-up page.

6. In-store

If you have a physical shop on the high street, this is a key place to encourage the opt-in at various points. This could be done with a separate positive opt-in alongside the form when people are signing in to use your free WIFI, posters in-store showing the benefits to joining the email programme, and most importantly, at the point of purchase.

Sign-up could be captured using an iPad for immediate sign-up or a paper sign-up form which is manually entered later in the day (although this leads to a delay in the process happening and errors are more likely to occur when manually typing in email addresses).

There are a whole variety of other places where you can encourage the sign-up – at events, in your personal email signature – anywhere that you have a touchpoint with your potential customers.

TAKE ACTION

Think about your current sign-up process, how you can improve what you have in place at the moment and how you can add to your current list growth strategy:

- What are your current data collection sources?

    Take note of every place you collect data for email marketing purposes and how this is formatted.

    o Are you collecting data from your website? If so, which types of form (for example, pop-ups, vs. footer pod vs. homepage call-out vs. blog post pod) see a higher conversion rate?

    o Do you have an app? If so, are you collecting data from app sign-ups?

    o Are you using the ability to sign up using a Facebook account?

    o Are you buying data? Or using affiliates to collect sign-ups?

    o Can customers sign up during the account creation/purchase process?

- Look at the source of your sign-ups:

    o Which see the highest engagement with your email campaigns? Which see the lowest?

    Consider statistics such as opens, clicks, unsubscribes, after what time period do subscribers stop interacting, complaints, average order value (AOV), number of transactions, revenue and lifetime value.

- o Which sources of data see the most and least opt-ins generated?

- Assess your current opt-in type – are you using single or double opt-in at each sign-up opportunity?

- Ultimately, how could you acquire more subscribers? Looking at all your current sign-up opportunities, evaluate their format and placement:

  - o Look at the offer that subscribers come in on – for example, are you offering a lead magnet (free download or percentage off their first order for example) vs. independently selling the benefits of receiving your emails?

  - o Take a look at your sign-up forms. Are they legally compliant? Are they clear in what the subscriber will receive and when from your brand?

  - o Evaluate the design of each sign-up opportunity (including the wording, colours and imagery used).

  - o Is there an additional incentive given to sign up – for example, 10% off your first order or a free download?

  - o What is your sign-up conversion rate through each instance on your website? (Which is the most effective at driving new sign-ups?)

  - o How could you optimise this? For example, the placement of forms on your website – what are the most visited/bounced pages on your site? How does your sign-up appear on these pages? Are you utilising all the areas you could be on site?

o   What's your current marketing strategy to drive traffic to your opt-ins? Are you running any paid ads? How much are you spending to gain an opt-in? Can this be optimised?

o   How could you optimise your post-sign-up journey?

See Appendix 8 on page 310 for example.

You can download a copy of this as a worksheet here: www.etelligencebook.com/members/step4/signup/

CHAPTER 5

REACH
Your Audience

Anyone currently running an email marketing programme will know that getting your emails delivered to the inbox is not always easy.

With obstacles not only blocking your path into the inbox but also the way your email is viewed and treated when it gets there, our job has become even tougher. Making sure your emails actually reach your subscribers is an ongoing task.

Your **delivery rate** is the number of people you send an email to, minus those that bounced (hard and soft bounces); it shows the number who received the email.

Your **Inbox Placement Rate (IPR)**, on the other hand, is the number of emails that actually reached the inbox as opposed to the junk folder, or being blocked by the mailbox provider and going 'missing'.

IPR cannot be seen in most ESPs without third-party technology also being used (such as that provided by companies like Return Path, for example).

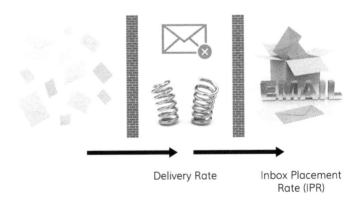

Delivery Rate   Inbox Placement Rate (IPR)

Deliverability is a complex and ever-changing topic, but this chapter will give you an introduction to some of the most important elements you need to look out for along the way.

5.1
Your Sender Reputation

An indicator of good deliverability is having a high **'sender reputation'**.

Your sender reputation is similar to an online credit score – it tells the receiving mailbox providers who you are and how good you are as a sender. If you have strong sending practices, you will have a high sender reputation, making you look good in the eyes of the mailbox providers and therefore increasing your deliverability.

Your sender score is presented as a score of between 0 and 100 and reflects your sender reputation. This score is based on various different elements including:

- **Your sending infrastructure**

  Your technical sending infrastructure is often the first thing that the mailbox providers (such as Microsoft, Oath and Gmail etc) look at when determining whether or not to deliver your emails. It lets them identify that you are who you say you are.

  Based on your sending domain and IP address, this includes elements such as:

  o **Reverse DNS (rDNS)** – determines the authenticity of a domain compared with the IP address it is originating from.

  o **DomainKeys Identified Mail (DKIM)** – the receiving Simple Mail Transfer Protocol (SMTP) server checks this digital signature (a private key that can only be used on the domain) against the public key for that domain and, if they are the same, the sender is authenticated as genuine.

- **Sender Policy Framework (SPF)** – an SPF record for the sender's (sub) domain confirms that the sending IP is allowed to send from that domain (by publishing a DNS record to show that the sender is genuine).

- **'Domain-based Message Authentication, Reporting and Conformance' (DMARC)** – builds on SPF and DKIM protocols, adding linkage to the author ('From:') domain name, published policies for recipient handling of authentication failures, and reporting from receivers to senders.

- **Transport Layer Security (TLS)** – this is a security protocol that encrypts email to protect its privacy.

- **Data quality**

  Your database should be kept clean by ensuring that unsubscribes, complaints, and hard bounces are immediately marked as non-contactable in your database. Soft bounces should also be removed after a number of consecutive occurrences (this ranges depending on your send strategy).

  - **Your complaint rate** – complaints are one of the biggest reasons for a drop in sender reputation and decreasing deliverability.

    There are many reasons why people complain about emails they receive, including receiving too many or too few emails, not recognising the brand, having a difficult or lengthy unsubscribe process in place, or they simply didn't understand what they were signing up to and when emails would be received.

    A complaint is recorded when a subscriber presses the 'spam' or 'junk' button in their email client in relation to your message.

    Some mailbox providers allow visibility for when this happens by allowing the sender to sign up for a 'feedback loop'. These allow you to receive messages back from subscribers who have complained. The mailbox provider forwards the message complained about back to your ESP at a designated email address that has been set up, primarily so that you can remove this subscriber from your list.

Unfortunately, not all mailbox providers give you the option for a feedback loop process to be set up. However, there are some that do. For example, Oath providers (including AOL and Yahoo!) as well as Gmail (this data is more valuable for high-volume senders) and Outlook.com (Hotmail). Your infrastructure is important here as DKIM is required in many cases for the feedback loop to work.

If you are generating complaints (and it doesn't take many to start causing deliverability issues – just 3 in 1,000 recipients) it is a good indication that something is not hitting the mark with your email programme.

In order to minimise complaints, it is important to provide targeted, relevant campaigns and deal with the reasons why people have chosen to click the spam/junk button to register a complaint.

Try focusing on some of the following elements to improve your complaint rates:

- Ensure you properly set expectations about your programme at point of sign-up.

- Make sure that your emails are what people expect to receive and are sent when they expect to receive them.

- Make it easier to unsubscribe than to complain.

  Remove those that unsubscribe from your list immediately. If someone has given you the benefit of the doubt and unsubscribed from your mailings, they may not do this again if they continue to receive communications from you and may reach for the spam/junk button to register a complaint. Additionally, ensure that you unsubscribe anyone who does register a complaint immediately.

Implement the list-unsubscribe function in your emails. This is an optional email header you can add to your messages – it is NOT your main unsubscribe link (this should still be included separately in the main body of your emails).

Using the list-unsubscribe function allows subscribers to see an additional unsubscribe button they can click if they would like to automatically stop receiving your emails. List-unsubscribe is used by Gmail, Outlook.com and others and is meant to help reduce complaints by giving subscribers a different method to safely unsubscribe, without negatively impacting your sending reputation. It can be implemented in two formats: the one-click list-unsubscribe and the mail-to list-unsubscribe.

– Send relevant, targeted content. Utilise the functionality available in most ESPs and the information you store about your subscribers to send triggered emails and dynamic content to plan and broadcast relevant email campaigns.

Implement a preference centre to find out what consumers want to receive from you and segment your list and communications accordingly, to provide highly relevant information (dynamic content will assist you enormously here). This could also be done through progressive profiling and inferred preferences based on a subscriber's behaviour (on site, through their purchases and with your email programme for example).

o **Unknown users** – these occur when a subscriber's email address is not recognised due to reasons such as the email address simply doesn't exist, or a typo was made on sign-up (also called a hard bounce).

As a general rule, if an email address hard bounces, it should immediately be removed from future sends. Broadcasts with a high number of unknown users/hard bounces can contribute to a drop in sender reputation.

As part of your technical infrastructure, you should have strong bounce processing procedures in place to remove these and other types of bounces.

In order to ensure the quality of your data, check email addresses on sign-up, either through the use of double opt-in (if your data source is more likely to be unreliable, such as affiliate marketing or other third-party sources as opposed to direct traffic to your website or landing page) or through email address validation.

o **Spam traps** – there are two types of spam trap to be aware of:

1. *Recycled spam traps:* some mailbox providers turn addresses that have shown no log-in activity for a long period of time (generally at least 12 months, but this can be much shorter – Gmail starts to be impacted when inactivity exceeds just 90 days, for example) into what are known as 'recycled spam traps'.

   By emailing subscribers that have been inactive for a long period of time, you run the risk of inadvertently emailing one of these reclaimed spam traps. To the mailbox providers, this is a sign of poor list hygiene and management.

2. ***Pristine spam traps*** – these are email addresses set up by mailbox providers and some blacklist providers, for example, specifically designed to catch senders who obtain addresses through data harvesting. These are a sign of poor list quality and questionable opt-in practices to the mailbox providers.

As painful as it is for most businesses to remove email addresses from their lists, there comes a point when there is a strong argument for inactive addresses to be removed from your sends in order to avoid hitting unknown users or recycled address spam traps.

Additionally, if you see a problem with spam traps, you should work towards identifying and removing them as soon as possible. These are extremely hard to identify down to a specific email address and therefore may involve removing small chunks of data as part of a strategic process. By doing so, you should see an increase in deliverability and IPR, which in turn could also lead to improved engagement rates.

- **Engagement with your campaigns**

The main method that mailbox providers use to determine whether or not incoming email is legitimate and wanted is by monitoring how engaged recipients are with your messages (your engagement rates). For example, do they open and read or delete and ignore messages they receive from you?

Engagement metrics are either deemed as positive or negative; if the mailbox providers see high positive engagement, future emails will be viewed more favourably, whereas a high negative engagement will have an adverse impact upon deliverability.

An important moment for the email industry occurred at the EEC's Email Evolution Conference 2015 in Florida. The question of what mailbox providers consider to be engagement indicators was put to a panel consisting of Gmail, AOL, Outlook (Microsoft), and Comcast, and they shared the following:

o Microsoft stated that user engagement will not affect a sender's overall reputation, and AOL and Gmail agreed with these statements.

o Comcast, however, said that engagement does affect overall reputation.

o For clarity, engagement will affect the ability to get to individual users' inboxes.

o Gmail stated that engagement will affect reputation in a positive reinforcement only.

o Gmail also stated that a signal from a user that something 'is not spam' is an order of magnitude more powerful than the spam button.

o Specific to Gmail, we also learnt there's a higher probability that someone will click the spam button if your email is in the 'primary' tab, but less likely for the 'promotions' tab. The message was 'Don't fight the tabs, they're a good thing'.

One thing all of the mailbox providers were clear on is they do not track clicks. This is mainly for privacy reasons, although there are also some technical reasons. The individual engagement metrics that they do consider are summarised in the table on the following page.

Engagement metric	Positive or negative
Opens	👍
Spam complaint	👎
Deleted without reading	👎
Filing (i.e. saving to another folder)	👍
Replying/forwarding	👍👍
Adding to the address book	👍
Retrieving emails from the junk folder	👍👍
Moving emails to the junk folder	👎
Deleted after reading (where rates are high)	👎

As can be seen here, engagement not only includes the standard metrics including opens and complaints, but more in-depth, 'hidden' metrics (based on how recipients interact further with communications that most ESPs do not report on, but third-party providers such as Return Path, amongst others, do). For example, the number of forwards, replies, deletions (with/without reading) and 'TINS' (this is not spam) actions that an email receives.

Even for email senders who do not have the ability to report against these metrics, there are steps you can take that will help to improve your programme's performance.

o **Deleted unread:** when emails are deleted unread, it usually indicates that recipients have not been persuaded by the offer presented in the subject line. Subject line testing is always recommended, and there are now solutions available that can be used to automate this process. Subscribers are also increasingly aware of email fraud, and are more predisposed to delete even legitimate emails that appear 'spammy'.

o **Deleted after reading:** potential causes may include when a compelling offer is not matched by the resulting offer or content when the email is opened, or the offer is not immediately visible.

o **Filing:** this is likely to happen when recipients are presented with valuable content that they want to reference at some point in the future – often seen with CRM emails (for example instructions or purchase information). You should consider approaches to include more of this type of content as part of your overall programme strategy – to increase this metric but also provide highly relevant and useful content for your subscribers.

o **Replying:** where two-way traffic is seen between sender and recipient, this represents dialogue and implies a genuine relationship between the two parties. This suggests you should not broadcast from an unattended address (i.e. noreply@) and that you should monitor inbound email traffic for genuine responses. You could also consider techniques to increase this behaviour (e.g. run a competition where replies need to go to this address).

o **Forwarding:** this will often happen when the email contains a viral element (e.g. a great offer, valuable content, humour) that predisposes recipients to share the email with friends, family and colleagues.

o **Add to address book:** some senders have started to move away from this approach, questioning the actual benefit it delivered, but the EEC feedback proves this is still valuable. In addition to having a request for this in every email, also make sure it forms part of the sign-up process, as well as the welcome and on-boarding series. Also consider having a web page with step-by-step instructions for each major mailbox provider.

o **Retrieve from junk:** many subscribers check their junk folders to search for emails they had expected to receive. It is important to ensure these emails stand out so they are easily visible to searchers. Emails that have been personalised with the recipient's name generally perform well, as do subject lines containing the sender's brand.

o **Moving emails to junk:** much of this comes down to subscriber trust. If you are a brand that your subscriber admires, you are providing them with perceived value, and you are honouring the commitments you made when they joined your email programme, therefore they will be far less likely to exhibit this behaviour. Again, personalisation can be beneficial (as long as it has been done correctly!) – people consider their names to be part of their personal inventory, and will be less likely to treat them in an abusive fashion.

o **The content you send**

Content still has a role to play in making sure that emails are delivered, as well as encouraging recipients to act on what they see. Not only should you be looking at how your messages render in different email clients (such as desktop or webmail vs. mobile devices) with images on and off, but also don't forget to look at the content of your messages that may trigger the spam filters including:

– large images
– a high image-to-text ratio
– number of spam words/phrases
– incorrect HTML coding

Cloudmark fingerprinting
Cloudmark provide anti-spam, phishing and virus protection to email providers covering over 1.6 billion mailboxes worldwide

and are a significant factor in getting your email delivered to your subscribers.

One of Cloudmark's anti-spam technology components is its advanced message fingerprinting – real-time algorithms that create fingerprints, or hashes, of various components of an email header, body and other characteristics.

When an email message is sent to a mailbox provider that uses Cloudmark's solutions, the filter:

— scans the entire email, which includes the header, subject line, body, and footer

— creates new fingerprints of content, URLs, images, and code

— compares the new fingerprints to the existing fingerprints in the Cloudmark database

— scores the similarity of fingerprints to messages considered to be spam or not-spam

— classifies the new fingerprints either as spam or not-spam based on its similarity to other messages in the Cloudmark database – and based on data received through Cloudmark's Global Threat Network

All messages sent to mailbox providers using Cloudmark's anti-spam solutions are fingerprinted, but not all fingerprints are considered spammy. If a message receives a spammy fingerprint, participating mailbox providers will use that as a factor in their filtering decisions. Usually, mailbox providers will place some of your email in the spam folder, or block your email completely depending on their individual filtering policies and other internal factors related to your sending reputation and sending history.

This means that even legitimate emails that look 'spammy' will likely experience deliverability problems.

Monitoring Tools to Help You Assess Your Deliverability

There are various tools available (free and paid) to help you assess factors that contribute to your sender score and therefore reputation, impacting your deliverability. These include:

1. Check your sender reputation by assessing your Sender Score at www.senderscore.org (provided by Return Path) – this will give you an idea of your current reputation standing.

2. Register for Microsoft's SNDS – www.sendersupport.olc.protection. outlook.com/snds/index.aspx

3. Gmail Postmaster Tools – www.gmail.com/postmaster/

These three tools will help you to gain a picture of how your email programme is being viewed by two of the biggest email providers and overall.

This will help you start to make decisions about elements of your programme that need to be changed to improve deliverability and your IPR. For example, if you have a high unknown user rate, you need to look at your bounce processing rules and data collection processes – validating addresses on sign-up and the quality of your data sources.

4. Email verification tools such as BriteVerify and FreshAddress to help you improve the quality of your data.

5. Tools to check for spam words/spam scores such as SpamAssassin, Postmark Spam Check and MailTester or Litmus and Email on Acid who also provide HTML validity testing and inbox preview tools.

6. Subject line testers such as Send Check It, Email Subject Line Grader, CoSchedule's Email Subject Line Tester, Zurb Subject Line Preview and Emotional Marketing Value Headline Analyzer.

7. Tools that check your technical infrastructure and blacklists such as MXToolbox and DNSstuff.

5.2
Your Sending IP Address

Sending from Shared vs. Dedicated IPs

When you send email marketing campaigns, you use a sending domain and an IP address to do so. When it comes to your sending IP address, you have two options: to use dedicated or shared IPs.

Dedicated IPs are those that are used by only you and no one else. This means that you have complete control over your sender reputation and the send volume is all your own and not slowed down by other senders or queued behind them.

Using dedicated IPs allows you to:

- more accurately pinpoint the source of any reputational problems and work to resolve them.

- ensure you don't get caught up in other senders' reputation problems.

- build your reputation as a sender – as a high-volume sender, you have the volume to be able to do this on your own and don't need to be propped up by other people's volume.

- segment critical mail streams onto separate IPs if you need to (for example, transactional vs. marketing). You may want to do this if you have large volumes of each being sent and want to ensure that your transactional emails are not slowed down by your marketing messages.

Shared IPs, on the other hand, are those that are shared and used not only by you, but other companies as well. You won't know who the other companies are, or what they are sending.

Using shared IPs is highly beneficial if you are not sending frequently or have a low volume (less than around 100,000 emails per week – at least 20k daily is really a minimum amount for a dedicated IP). In order to build a sender reputation, you need to have at least this amount of volume sending over your IP, so if you have less than this, you can create an amalgamated reputation by joining with other senders in this way.

It also means that everyone benefits from the positive engagement generated by each company, however the flip side of the coin is that everyone is also impacted by their negative engagement as well – so if another company on the same IP infrastructure generates a high complaint rate and your emails are sending at this time, you could get caught in any negative impact from this.

Using and Warming a New IP Address to Send From

An IP address that is new and hasn't been used before (and domain if using a new domain) has no sender reputation and so you need to get the mailbox providers used to you sending to them.

You should start by sending to your most engaged data (for example, those who have opened your emails in the last 30 days) and slowly ramp up the volume of your sends per day over a couple of months, so the ISPs can get used to what you send, when, and the volume you send. When it comes to deliverability, open is the key metric by which you can segment around engagement – as previously mentioned, click rates are not considered by the mailbox providers.

It is not widely published for most what they will accept, but as an example, Microsoft (Hotmail) will typically only accept around 4k per day for an IP with no reputation.

It is a common spam practice to send a large volume of emails infrequently. Make sure you don't fall into this cycle and keep a regular, consistent volume being sent from your IPs.

When starting to use a new ESP and therefore setting up new IPs, migrating from shared to dedicated IPs or simply adding new IPs into your rotation to send from, there are some key tasks you need to complete:

- Decide on the number of IPs you want to use. Don't use too many or mailbox providers may mark you as a snowshoe spammer: this phrase describes the technique that spammers use to evade filters and get around reputation metrics by spreading their output across multiple domains and IPs; this could be compared to how a snowshoe works by spreading a person's load across a wide area of snow.

- Decide on your IP structure – segmented by email engagement for example (high risk data vs. highly engaged data) or email type (marketing communications vs. CRM transactional emails). Not all ESPs will allow you this flexibility and some may only allow you to use multiple IPs in a round-robin format (where your send volume is split over multiple IPs).

- Design your engagement data segmentation – define and create segments to use during the warm-up process (starting with your most engaged data to build your reputation).

- Create your IP warm-up strategy – this includes how much volume will be sent, when and for how long to complete your warm-up.

- Start your warm-up process – monitor the warm-up process and make live adjustments to segment (overall/per mailbox provider) as you go, dependent on results.

  Continue the warm-up until you reach your required volume or the point at which IPR cannot be any further improved. For example, there may come a point in your warm-up where you have introduced older engagement data and your IPR starts to drop – in this case you need to decide what to do with this remaining volume (such as re-permission or removing subscribers from future sends).

- Keep a backup of sends going on your current infrastructure while going through the warm-up to ensure full volume sends are still possible.

- Complete your warm-up and resume normal send segmentation.

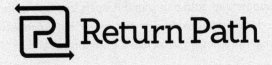

CASE STUDY

Return Path

Client Type: Platform for social change

Objective: To ensure their advocates receive and can immediately act on each message.

Situation

Change.org operates the world's largest platform for social change with thousands of campaigns created each day by users looking to effect change. To help these petitions succeed, Change.org uses email to connect each petition to over 180 million advocates around the world. From alerts about a new petition and updates on an ongoing cause to a last-minute call for additional support, every email is crucial. To ensure their advocates receive and can immediately act on each message, Change.org needed a way to ensure that their email would reach the inbox and render perfectly.

Challenges

Every message that is not delivered to the inbox leaves a cause unsupported. To maximise and protect their deliverability, Change.org needed deeper insight into where their email was being delivered and why. But simply reaching the inbox is not enough. With advocates in every country of the world, Change.org also needs to ensure that every email will open perfectly, regardless of which of the many international email platforms their advocates use.

> *'For us, making sure that our millions of users engage with the campaigns on our site is essential to our success. Inbox Monitor helps us ensure our mail is reaching our users and getting to their inboxes and driving that engagement.'*
>
> Alice Cornell, Director of Email Deliverability

Solution

Email is a uniquely powerful tool in the fight for change, so landing in the inbox is essential. Using Return Path's Inbox Monitor, Change.org is able to follow each email from send to delivery, allowing them to immediately identify if and when their messages are diverted to the spam folder. Knowing this allows Change.org to immediately react and resolve any deliverability issues, ensuring that future messages – and the causes they support – will reach advocates who can help.

Arriving in the inbox is only the first step. Change.org also needed to ensure the design of each message would render correctly, no matter where it was opened. A poorly rendered email not only presents a poor user experience, but it diminishes the true purpose of the message – connecting advocates to worthy causes and providing them with the tools to support change. Using Inbox Preview, Change.org is able to confirm the layout of each campaign on multiple devices and web browsers before hitting 'Send'. Now, no matter which browser, platform, or device an advocate uses, every message will open flawlessly, highlighting important causes in need of support.

With Return Path's solutions, Change.org has achieved near perfect inbox placement at its four key mailbox providers. The dynamic visibility into their campaign performance has also enabled Change.org to increase their campaign sends each month while maintaining their strong deliverability – connecting each cause to more supporters. As Alice Cornell confirms, 'Email is at the heart of our mission. Email is what helps our users drive their campaigns and helps us share their inspiring stories with other users.'

✎ TAKE ACTION

- Ascertain your current delivery rate

- Consider the third-party tools available to help you monitor your Inbox Placement Rate

  o Monitor your Sender Score

  o Ensure all the elements of your sending infrastructure are in place (consider using a tool such as MXToolbox to check some of these elements)

- Monitor your data quality (unknown user rate, complaint rate etc.)

- Consider the positive and negative engagement metrics (you are able to track)

- As per Chapter 1.6, analyse whether you have seen any increases or decreases in these metrics over time

- Register for the following free tools to help assess your deliverability (as well as any paid tools you are able to access):

  o Check your sender reputation by assessing your Sender Score at www.senderscore.org (provided by Return Path) – this will give you an idea of your current reputation standing.

  o Register for Microsoft's SNDS – www.sendersupport.olc.protection.outlook.com/snds/index.aspx

  o Gmail Postmaster Tools – www.gmail.com/postmaster/

- Consider whether shared or dedicated IPs might be the best option for your business

You can find out more here:

www.etelligencebook.com/members/step5/deliverability/

Email marketing isn't dead, the way you're using it is...

...not anymore!

Now that you've reached the end of the book, you should...

- have conducted an audit of your current strategy to give you a clear view of where you are coming from.

- know how to optimise what you're currently doing.

- have a plan of how you will move forward to increase the ROI of your campaigns over the next 6-12 months.

- have an understanding of the importance of consistently growing your email list with quality data and the elements that impact your conversion rates.

- have an idea of the key elements affecting your deliverability.

But the work doesn't end here!

We've only just scratched the surface of what's possible for you and your email marketing.

Keep learning, testing, analysing, and most of all, keep implementing!

Good luck!

Kate

Don't forget to jump online and get your free resources in your E-telligence online membership site!

Simply go to www.etelligencebook.com/ and register using the code **'ETELLIGENCE'** to gain access.

Acknowledgements

First and foremost, I'd like to say a massive thank you to my husband Chris and son Jack, without whose support and encouragement the writing of this book would not have been possible.

I'd also like thank you the following organisations who sponsored this book and provided such informative case studies to help illustrate some of the elements discussed:

About

eFOCUS
Marketing

Kate Barrett is the founder of **eFocus Marketing**, a specialist email marketing agency based in London.

The eFocus Marketing team provides a dedicated email marketing resource to companies looking to optimise, automate and grow their email marketing programme.

From strategic consulting, to full service management and training, we address every aspect of an email programme to produce successful campaigns.

Our team of experts will work out the best options for your business and offer solutions in bite-size pieces so that you can focus on quick wins that will increase your success as well as longer term changes to become a better sender and increase your results.

Get in touch!
www.e-focusmarketing.com
enquiries@e-focusmarketing.com
01689 897 592

Twitter: @efocus_marketin
Facebook.com/efocusmarketing
Linkedin.com/in/katebarrettonline

Appendices

Appendix 1

	Business goal	Email marketing goal(s)	Tactics
1	Increase sales	Increase first purchase sales	Customer journey stage: consideration
		Individual campaign goals • Increase open rate • Increase click rate • Increase conversion rate	**Manual campaigns:** Send weekly promotional emails to highlight special offers, inspire subscribers and advertise key products and categories Personalise recommendations
			Triggered campaigns: Abandoned basket

Actions	Results
Sent every Tuesday and Thursday at 8am Includes product recommendations and any special promos that are happening (e.g. 10% off) Personalised based on interests and behaviour data (website browse data) A/B split test performed on each send (GOAL: changes with each send – e.g. increase click rate) Marketing team to build and send weekly Segmentation: content changes depending on whether they have previously made a purchase – some offers are different and based on previous purchase behaviour if they have	Track delivery rate, unique opens, clicks, open-to-click rate, complaints and conversions to purchase Main metric: conversion rate and revenue generated
Set up in ESP by marketing team Triggered based on items left in basket for more than 1 hour Contains recap of items left in basket (up to 3 items) and a prompt to re-purchase Recommendations for other products that may be suitable based on basket items	Track delivery rate, unique opens, clicks, open-to-click rate, complaints and conversions to purchase Main metric: conversion rate and revenue generated

Appendix 2

Priority ranking	Data type	Data field	How is this data collected?
1	Purchase data	Last product(s) purchased – name	Tracked purchase behaviour
2	Purchase data	Last product(s) purchased – price	Tracked purchase behaviour
3	Purchase data	Last product(s) purchased – description	Tracked purchase behaviour
4	Known data	Customer name (first name)	Sign-up form/purchase process/account sign-up process

Where is this data stored?	Is it currently available for use in your email marketing campaigns?	How is this data currently used in your campaigns?
eCommerce system	Yes	To personalise product recommendations In review emails
eCommerce system	Yes	
eCommerce system	No	
eCommerce system and ESP	Yes	To personalise all communications (e.g. Hi first name)

Appendix 3

TYPE	Description	Trigger	Rules
Transactional emails	Order confirmation email	Making a purchase	Sent to every purchaser
Lead-nurturing emails	Welcome email and on-boarding series	Prospect registers to receive email marketing via website form	Only sent to new subscribers Remove from standard campaign sends until day eight post-sign-up Stops if user purchases
Behaviour-based emails	Abandoned basket series	Subscriber leaves products in their basket	Takes precedence over all other campaigns (other than purchase emails) Stops if user purchases

Timing	Outline	Purpose of the email	Live?
Sent immediately after a purchase made	Confirms the order and details Outlines next steps (e.g. delivery) Offers upsell opportunities	To confirm the order has been placed, what was in the order and how to contact the company if there is a problem	Yes
1. Immediately post-sign-up 2. One day post-sign-up 3. Three days post-sign-up 4. Seven days post-sign-up 5. Ten days post-sign-up 6. Thirteen days post-sign-up	1. Welcome email 2. Intro key product categories 3. Highlight app download 4. Latest bestselling products (based on browse behaviour) 5. Highlight social media channels 6. Latest trending products	To welcome the subscriber and introduce them to the brand and key aspects of the website – encourage a first purchase	Yes
2 hours after basket abandoned 24 hours later 48 hours later	Did you forget something? We've still got your basket saved – you may also like our recommendations Do you need any help?	Encourage the subscriber back to purchase items in their basket/suggest alternatives	Yes

Appendix 4

Segmentation criteria	Content ideas

Ease of implementation (1-10 – 10 being easiest to implement)	Potential impact (1-10 – 10 being highest impact)	Total

Appendix 5

Email # in series	Timing	Topic	Conversion
1	Immediately after sign-up	Welcome and thank new subscribers. Deliver opt-in offer. Lead them through to key categories of products	Click to explore product categories
2	One day later	Why use your brand (brand story/ five reasons why etc.)	Click to explore specific products
3	3 days later	Highlight app download	Click to download app
4	3 days later	Latest bestselling products	Links to individual products
5	3 days later	Connect with us on social media	Links to social media channels
6	3 days later	Latest trending products	Links to individual products

Notes	Exclusions
Tailor welcome email content to the offer the subscriber came in on, data source and any other information you have that differentiates the subscriber at this stage.	
Track clicks from email one and tailor product recommendations based on categories they showed interest in through this behaviour/website browse behaviour since sign-up. If no behavioural activity to base this on, highlight key categories or top-selling products – use dynamic content to keep these suggestions current.	Don't trigger if a subscriber has made a purchase/is part of the abandoned cart series.
How to shop on the app and why it's beneficial to download – e.g. how it makes shopping easier, save your favourites etc.	
Based on browse behaviour if possible. If not, bestselling/top trending products.	
No more than three channels.	
Based on browse behaviour if possible. If not, bestselling/top trending products.	

Appendix 6

Campaign description
Ongoing, documented testing strategy
Welcome and on-boarding programme
Optimisation of sign-up form

Ease of implementation (1-10 – 10 being easiest to implement)	Potential impact (1-10 – 10 being highest impact)	Total score
7	9	16
6	8	14
5	5	10

Appendix 7

	Acquisition and discovery stage	Research and consideration stage
Tasks		
Questions		
Touchpoints		
Emotions		
Weaknesses		

Purchase and experience stage	Loyalty and repeat purchase stage	Reactivation stage

Appendix 8

Place shown on website	Conversion rate to opt-in
Homepage – time-delayed pop-up	30%

Wording used	Opt-in type	Opt-in offer
Get our weekly email sent straight to your inbox and be the first to know about our latest deals, exclusive subscriber offers, trends and much more!	Positive single opt-in (e.g. positive single opt-in/double opt-in/soft opt-in; not recommended and in many cases, not legally compliant)	10% off your first order when you subscribe

References

1   p. 9 DMA Email Marketer Tracker Report 2018
https://dma.org.uk/uploads/misc/5a7c1de1ca4d7-marketer-email-tracking-report-2018_v2-final_5a7c1de1ca425.pdf

2   p. 43 MailChimp, 2017
www.mailchimp.com/resources/effects-of-list-segmentation-on-email-marketing-stats/

3   p.44 Pure360
www.pure360.com/email-marketing-statistics/

4   p. 51 Campaign Monitor
www.campaignmonitor.com/resources/infographics/24-email-marketing-stats-need-know/

5   p.81 Litmus – State of Email Workflows
www.litmus.com/ebooks/state-of-email-workflows-2018

6   p. 118 Ascend2, 2016
www.ascend2.com/wp-content/uploads/2017/01/Ascend2-Email-Marketing-Strategy-Survey-Summary-Report-160908.pdf

7   p. 125 Internet Retailer
www.digitalcommerce360.com/internet-retailer/

8   p. 125 Fresh Relevance
www.freshrelevance.com/blog/6-simple-steps-to-increase-your-sales-36-using-fresh-relevance

9   p. 177 Optimizely
        www.optimizely.com/optimization-glossary/statistical-
        significance/

10   p. 207 Demand Gen Report's '2016 Lead Scoring Survey'
        www.demandgenreport.com/resources/reports/the-2016-lead-
        scoring-survey-report

11   p. 208 BlueHornet, 2013
        www.slideshare.net/bluehornetemail/bluehornet-consumer-
        views-of-email-marketing-2013-presentation-final

12   p. 208 Return Path, 2015
        www.returnpath.com/newsroom/email-marketers-welcome-
        messages-drive-predict-subscriber-engagement-return-path-
        study/

13   p. 208 Easy-SMTP, 2015
        www.easy-smtp.com/welcome-email-marketing-optimization
        2015